Sort of Okay, Sort of Not

HOW TO MAKE SENSE OF YOUR 20S, WHILE YOU'RE STILL MAKING SENSE OF YOURSELF.

Nathan Moss

Published by Uncle Nathan
Sydney, Australia

ISBN: 978-1-7646074-1-4
eISBN: 978-1-7646074-0-7

First Edition, 2026

Cover photography by Remy Gavagna.
Interior formatting by Author Services Australia.

www.unclenathan.com

For everyone who's ever felt like they're figuring it out as they go—
because you are, and that's exactly how it's supposed to be.

Contents

SOMEWHERE BETWEEN LOST AND FIGURING IT OUT

Read This Before You Read Anything Else

If you picked up this book thinking it would give you all the answers - sorry, but you're in the wrong place. This isn't a step-by-step guide to "finding yourself." It's not a motivational pep talk telling you to wake up at 5am and manifest your dream life. And it sure as hell isn't written by someone who's got it all figured out.

This book is Messy. Honest. Raw. And at times, uncomfortable.

Because that's what life actually is in your 20s.

Confusing. Contradictory. Beautiful. Terrifying.

All at once.

I didn't write this book from the top of the mountain. I wrote it while still climbing, slipping, second-guessing, and honestly, wondering if I was even on the right mountain in the first place. But, that's why this book exists. Because somewhere along the way, I realised that the most valuable thing I could offer wasn't a blueprint for life, it was simply some company in the chaos of it all. So, if you're in the thick of it right now, feeling like you're falling behind, questioning who the hell you even are or supposed to be, comparing your life to everyone else's highlight reel, wondering if you're the only one still figuring it out…

You're not.

Welcome to the club.

This book is for you.

Why I Wrote This

When I started sharing bits of my life online - stories, thoughts, lessons I'd learned the hard way - I didn't expect anyone to care. I was just some guy in his early 20s trying to make sense of things out loud. But then something weird happened… people started replying:

"I feel the exact same way."
"Mate... it's like you're in my head."
"Thank you for putting this into words for me."

That's when I realised something important - we're all feeling the same things, but nobody's *really* talking about it. No one wants to admit they're lost. Or insecure. Or anxious. Or behind. So we all pretend. We all perform. We project curated versions of our lives and call it connection. But deep down, we're all just craving one thing: to feel understood. I didn't write this book to give you all the answers. I wrote it to remind you that you're not broken for asking the questions.

The truth is, I can't promise this book will fix anything. But I can promise this:

By the time you finish it, you'll feel less alone in the confusion you've been quietly carrying.

And sometimes, that feeling is enough to change everything.

Who This Book Is For

If you're in your 20s and feel like you should have your shit together by now, but don't…

this book is for you.

If you're scared of making the wrong decision because you don't know what the right one is…

this book is for you.

If you're working hard but still feel like you're behind everyone else…

this book is for you.

Or, if you're just looking for something honest, something real, something that sounds like a conversation with your older brother, your best mate, or the voice in your head when the noise dies down…

this book is for you too.

What's Actually Inside

Each chapter dives into a specific part of the chaos that is early adulthood - from relationships, self-worth and mental health, to careers, identity and the pressure to always be "doing more." It's not written in a polished, perfect way, because well, life is far from polished and perfect. It's told through real stories, vulnerable moments, things I've messed up, things I've learned, and a lot of reflection in between.

Think of this book like a journal you weren't meant to read - except I published it on purpose.

It isn't just me ranting about my feelings, though. Every chapter goes deeper than my words alone. Alongside my own stories, you'll find references to psychology studies, scientific findings, philosophical frameworks, and expert insights. These aren't there to make the book feel "academic," they're there because sometimes we need someone else, someone who has studied this stuff for decades, to give us the words that describe why we feel the way we do.

Here's the catch though: this isn't a traditional book you just passively read front to back. This book wants something from you. Each chapter ends with **space to write, reflect or explore**. There are prompts. Questions. Blank pages that you can ignore if you want to, but could change the way you see yourself if you don't. Because I didn't write this book just for you to read it. I wrote it to start a conversation with yourself. If you're brave enough to have it, I promise it'll be worth it.

How to Read This Book

You don't have to go in order. Some chapters might hit you harder than others. Some might not feel relevant until later. That's okay. This isn't school. You're not getting tested at the end. Read what you need. Skip what you don't.

More importantly: **pause when something hits you.**

Take a second. Write a note. Scribble in the margins. Highlight the hell out of it. Take a photo and send it to a friend. Let it sit with you. And if you don't want to do any of that, that's okay too. But here's what I will ask of you: don't read this with a filter. Don't try to be "better" while you're reading it. Come as you are. Raw. Confused. Brilliant. Imperfect. Wholeheartedly *you* and no one else. This book was written that way. It deserves to be read that way too.

One Last Thing Before We Start

You don't need to have everything figured out to live a life that matters.

You don't need a five-year plan.

You don't need to be constantly grinding or proving yourself.

You just need to be human.

That's it.

Messy. Flawed. Real.

If this book does anything at all, I hope it reminds you that you're not behind. You're not broken. You're not failing just because things feel hard right now.

You're growing. And yes, sometimes growth looks like overthinking every decision at 2am, or crying for no reason in the middle of the week, or feeling like everyone else is doing better than you. But it's still growth. You're still moving forward. So don't rush through it. Let it unfold. Let it stretch you. Let it humble you. Let it teach you. Because that's where life really happens.

Okay, now let's begin.

Part 1

THE REAL WORLD IS A LIE

Chapter 1

SCHOOL SCREWED YOU

We spend the first two decades of our lives being told that school is the key to success. That if we just follow the rules, get good grades, and do what we're told, life will somehow fall into place. It's comforting, in a way - the structure, the routine, the clear path to what feels like progress. But then you leave school, and the real world doesn't hand you a syllabus. There's no cheat sheet for life, no predetermined path. You're left with this vast, confusing freedom, and it's easy to wonder: what on earth was all that for?

And, I think that's what messes with us. Not the pressure to succeed. But the whiplash of thinking we were doing everything right, only to realise the rules were made for a game we're not even playing anymore. The truth is, school doesn't prepare you for the chaos of the real world. It teaches you how to follow rules, but not how to build your own rules, or navigate a life where there aren't any. And as it turns out, this isn't just our experience, there's actual research to back it up.

A well-known NASA study found that 98% of 5-year-olds were testing at "creative genius" levels, yet by adulthood only 2% were still there. Quite literally, as we go through school our natural creativity gets schooled out of us.

This chapter dives into that disconnect - the system that shapes us for so long, only to leave us feeling completely unprepared for the world it's supposed to 'ready' us for.

. . .

I was 13 and already over school.

It wasn't that I hated it; I just loved school holidays more. The idea of five more years of uniforms and routines felt like a life sentence when all I wanted was freedom. It was also around this time in my life when my parents would repeatedly say 'Enjoy it, buddy! When you're finished, you'll wish you were back there!' and while I never really understood what they meant back then, I'm beginning to understand it a bit better now.

Every kid has a natural inclination to hate school - even if they actually love it. See, I loved school because it was made for people like me. It gave me structure and told me what to do every day, and I thrived in that environment. But I wasn't going to admit that - not to myself or anyone else. Even though I was achieving top of my class in subjects I enjoyed, DUX of my year group, sport awards and accolades, recognition from teachers, and the rest of it, I genuinely believed that school sucked and I was the only unlucky kid who had to suffer through it.

Truth is, I thrived in school, and I still hated it. It felt like the one thing standing between me and the freedom I was so desperate for. The freedom to wake up and not be ready by 7:30am for the school bus, the freedom to play video games for 8 hours if I wanted to, the freedom to eat lunch at 12:53 pm instead of 1:10 pm every day, the freedom to jump on my pushbike and go for a surf in the middle of the day, the freedom to choose what I do and when I do it.

It's ironic. The freedom I craved back then is now the same freedom that stresses me out as an adult. It's not that I don't love having choices - it's just that I'm now the one responsible for making them. When my parents would say 'you'll wish you were back there' maybe they were actually trying to tell me to enjoy the routine, the structure, the predetermined layout of every day, week, term and year. Maybe it's not school itself, but rather, the system that I was forced to accept, that I miss so dearly.

With every passing year, from the age of 13 and even today, this structure that I grew so dependent on, continues to dictate my life. In Year 8, the only decisions left up to me were what to do with my Saturday afternoon after football, and what to do with my Sunday - and even then, mum or dad usually had pre-booked plans for me anyway. I also got to choose what I wanted to do with my free time after school but that was basically one of three things - football training, PlayStation, or jump on the trampoline in my front yard.

In Year 10, I moved to Jindabyne for 1 semester to live at boarding school and snowboard as part of an elite training program called ESA (Elite Snowsports Academy). This was a big step for an excited 16-year-old Nathan who had grown so used to his normal routine. I was now living in an unfamiliar place, with unfamiliar people, and an even more rigorous routine.

It's funny, I had total freedom in being away from my parents, and yet, none at all in the strict regime of boarding school. I loved it, even though I convinced myself I didn't - once again, feeling like my freedom was hindered. Now I didn't have to make any decisions at all. They were essentially made for me every day. I was given the illusion of responsibility in that I had to wake up, eat toast and be ready by 5:30am for the bus up the mountain, but even if I wasn't, there was always going to be an adult nearby to wake me up and get me ready. I had my 4 hours of snowboarding in the morning, then I had my core subjects at school, followed by 4 hours of tutoring at night, and then I would sleep and repeat. On the weekends, our schedule was determined by whichever activities our boarding house supervisors had planned, and being under 17, I wasn't allowed to leave unless I was signed out by a guardian. I grew bored of the system that made life so easy for me. And with that boredom, I grew resentful. I was trying to think of ways to escape the routine. Anything to give me a true sense of freedom, a real feeling of responsibility - and I found it. My first love...

She was older and I thought she was really fun, and she lived in Jindabyne, which meant her parents could sign me out of the boarding house on the weekend and give me that freedom I was oh so desperate for. Sorted. After 4 long weeks of being stuck in the boarding house, I walked out of those gates on a sunny Saturday morning, feeling like I'd found my freedom.

And, by Sunday morning, I had no idea what to do with it. So, inevitably, I resorted back to the routine I had grown so accustomed to. I got ready, I had some toast, I walked back to the boarding house and got on the bus ready for weekend training. Even though I now had the choice to go up the mountain later, or not at all, I still chose to follow the routine that I blamed for taking away my freedom.

Maybe freedom isn't what I longed for after all...

. . .

I was 17 now and had just started at a new high school to finish Year 11 and 12. It was a senior high school dedicated to supporting students in their final 2 years of school, with all emphasis on achieving the results you wanted to achieve without the distraction of younger year groups. Great for those who had high expectations - aka me.

For anyone unaware, in NSW we use the ATAR system to rank each student graduating from high school in a given year group across all the schools in the state. You have to complete certain minimum hours and prerequisite units to be eligible and then after your final High School Certificate (HSC) exams, you're given your ATAR ranking, with the best possible ranking being 99.95 (or in other words, in the top 0.05% of the state). This ATAR ranking is basically your ticket into university.

For the course I was eyeing off at the University of Technology, Sydney, I needed a minimum ATAR of 90, so basically, I needed to rank in the top 10% to get a guaranteed offer. Being a chronic overachiever, I decided to set myself the goal of graduating with an ATAR of 96 - just to prove to myself (and subconsciously prove to others) that I could do better than 90. The thing about this ranking system is that it boils down to a predetermined criteria - a fixed number of students, a max score for each exam, and a clear way to measure how much better or worse you are than everyone else in your age group across the state, and because of this, it becomes a competition with an objective and a tangible understanding of what it will take to be the best.

From this point on, my marks mattered and I was fully aware of the game I was playing. So I began on my quest to be the best. I did everything right - studied hard, aced exams, listened in class. I understood the assignment, so to speak. And I was rewarded for my hard work. I was getting exam marks above 90% in most subjects, I was ranked in the top 5 for most of my classes, and I was ready to sit the final exams, albeit with an enormous expectation on myself to perform.

With the pressure building and the time coming to sit my HSC exams, I grew tired of studying and just wanted the year to be over. I burnt out hard just before exams and in my eyes, I flunked them. Not flunked as in "I got 45%," but I definitely got results more consistent with students who were in the middle of their class rather than in the top 5. It stung.

I got an ATAR of 94 in the end.

I got into my course at uni without any dramas.

I got awards for being top of my class.

I got awards for my extracurricular activities.

In fact, I was awarded 'Best All-Rounder' at our graduation assembly.

Top 5 in Economics, Business Studies, Geography, Best All-Rounder, Leadership in Sports Award, Gold Merit Award, and of course, a graduation certificate.

And yet, despite all of these achievements, I felt like I had failed...

The top 6% of the state wasn't the top 4%, and that hurt my ego more than I wanted to admit.

Turns out, it's painfully common to tie your self-worth to those external markers of success. Psychologists actually have a term for it: "socially prescribed perfectionism," meaning your worth depends on meeting others' expectations. One long-term study found this type of perfectionism in young people has shot up 33% since the late 1980s, which has gone hand-in-hand with rising anxiety and depression rates.

It's funny, from the minute we start our schooling, to the minute we finish it, everything revolves around marks and rankings. Even in kindergarten, if you call the image of an Apple an Orange, you bet you're on notice as one who may need a bit more help and you'll probably be put in the 'lower ability' group. It's crazy to me that we can receive a mark of 9/10 and think we failed because it doesn't say 10/10 - like 100% (aka PERFECT) is the only acceptable result. We are conditioned to focus on the mistakes we make rather than the successes we achieve.

So, when I finally made it to the end and my marks didn't add up to the expectation I had based on the marks I had been receiving for the past 13 years, I felt like I had failed. And the point I'm getting at here isn't actually anything to do with my own mental state. No, it's much deeper than that. I'm trying to show you just how programmed we are to think about everything as if we were taking an exam, long after we've walked out of those high school gates for good.

. . .

Fast forward to university and I was experiencing the same thing. I had been given the course outline, I had some direction in terms of what it would take to pass my subjects, and I had the assumption in my head that I needed to get decent results to land a good job at the end of it all. Again, university became all about my marks. I didn't actually care so much for learning the content, I just needed to know enough to pass my subjects and get my degree - this was my thinking.

After studying hard in high school to achieve great marks, I had realised that maybe this time around I should try working smarter, not harder.

So, that's exactly what I did. I showed up, skimmed the course outlines, and figured out what I needed to know to pass. Nothing more, nothing less. I didn't buy 1 single textbook during my 3 years of university. I went only to the mandatory classes (and even skipped some in the end), and I completed quite literally the bare minimum requirements to pass the subject with an attractive enough mark for potential future employers.

I graduated with a distinction average, I think... to be honest, I left uni before I had even graduated. I moved overseas with no intention of using my degree. I got my degree sent to me virtually and I think I opened it maybe once or twice in the week I got it but I haven't looked at it again since. Nor have I looked at my ATAR since the day I was accepted into university - and I'm sure you're the same in that regard.

Without this overarching feeling that my marks would determine my future, I began to realise that they really didn't mean shit. Like I said, my marks were only a reflection of my ability to learn what was necessary for each exam. They didn't represent my ability to think creatively, or my capacity for new knowledge, or my aptitude for problem solving. They simply measured how well I followed the course outline based on what the people who wrote the course thought was necessary for you to be considered educated in that field.

With this newfound sense of freedom, I came to understand that my marks did not matter. I was lost. I'd spent the last 16 years believing my marks were everything and that success was just a matter of routine and following orders. So, if school wasn't giving me the freedom I wanted, and my marks weren't the key to my future, what was the point of it all? And why did it take me so long to ask this question?

The thing about the adult world is that there is no curriculum. There is no predetermined structure, or routine, or plan for each person. It's actually up to us to decide what to do with our day, what step to take next, what direction to follow - and it's this freedom to choose that causes so many problems for us.

Let me be clear, this is not an attack on teachers, nor is it an attack on any one person or party involved in the current system. This is simply me noticing a huge lag in the way our system should operate to prepare today's generation for the modern world of work. Sure, 50 years ago, a strict routine and an expectation for excellence made sense. It made sense because a large majority of the population were being groomed to work as an employee in a factory with a bottom line and quotas to meet.

This just simply isn't the case anymore. The world of work as we know it is dynamic, it's creative, it's constantly evolving and it sure as hell is not nice to anyone who thinks they can get by without adaptation.

I mean, take this as an example: the World Economic Forum predicts about 65% of children entering primary school now will end up working in jobs that don't even exist yet. That's how fast things are changing. No wonder there's often a gap between school and the "real world."

The truth is - our school system did fail us, and continues to fail us in so many ways. Granted, we learn to think for ourselves and problem solve on a basic level, we learn to comprehend large numbers and complex problems, but, we could still learn all of those things in a much more multifaceted environment than the one we are forced to abide by today.

The adult world does not rank us based on our results compared to the other people who were born within the same year as we were. The adult world does not give us a predetermined routine and schedule. The adult world does not give us a specific criteria for success in any given field. The adult world simply forces us to figure things out for ourselves and requires us to try, and fail, before we learn anything at all.

Unlike school, we are given many opportunities to learn and test our knowledge. You don't get just one chance to learn something. You don't rely on just one result to take a step forward. You are repeatedly tested, every single day, and you are rewarded for trying, not for succeeding. In fact, oftentimes we learn so much more from 'failure' than we do from success and that is where I think school has let us down. We were made to believe that a great mark means great work, and that is true - but a poor mark doesn't always mean poor work. It may simply mean you were looking in the wrong place, or that particular thing just isn't for you. The point is - school is too black and white, and sadly, it sucks the colour from anyone who doesn't fit the black and white system. Imagine if our awards assembly rewarded students in the grade who attempted the most new things over the year, or students who asked the most questions - these are the students who are more likely to succeed in the adult world - not me, who got rewarded simply for studying the right parts of the textbook...

Luckily for us, it's not all doom and gloom just because school didn't teach us how to choose our own routine or strive for our own version of success. The fact is, we have to unlearn the false truth that there is a right way to achieve success, to then understand that success looks different for every person, in every field, and at every stage of life. Success can be academic and professional, but it can also be deeply personal and emotional. Our fixation on finding the perfect linear path to adult success simply will not work. There is no single version of a 'Billionaire's Routine for Success' playbook. There are simply insights, opportunities, and room for growth.

So, once I realised that what brought me success in school wouldn't work for me in the adult world, I had to rethink my approach and get comfortable with the following:

1. No one is going to give you an optimal routine for your goals - you need to set your goals and then make small adjustments to your routine until you find yourself getting closer to those goals. This process will never stop. Your routine will always be changing.
2. No one can accurately tell you whether what you are doing is right or wrong - they will try, but where one may say you're doing it right, another will say you're doing it wrong. You need to look at the real (and usually convoluted) results yourself to determine whether you are progressing or not.

Let me make this clear,
your focus should be on progression, not perfection.

And that last line is something that has helped me tremendously with the fear of the unknown - your focus should be on progression, not perfection - because the truth is, there is no final destination. Life's not about reaching the peak; it's about getting comfortable with the climb, and with this in mind, we should be more concerned with our next step in that journey, rather than what the top of the mountain might look like.

Not so quick...

Now, this definitely isn't the part where I tell you to "write three things you're grateful for."

But, if something stuck from this chapter, if a belief was challenged, or a certain thought made an impact - this is where you might want to take a second to reflect on it.

Write it down if you want to, or just sit with it for a few seconds.

Is What I Know Actually So?

Think back to one thing school gave you praise for - an exam mark, an award, a presentation.

Now finish this sentence:

That moment made me believe that success meant ____________________.

Then, ask yourself:

Do I still believe that? Maybe this belief no longer serves me...

Chapter 2

SUCCESS KINDA SUCKS

You know the feeling. You set your sights on a big goal, work your ass off to get there, and when you finally reach it, you're left thinking:

"Really, that's it?"

Society has conditioned us to believe that ticking off life's milestones - graduating, getting a good job, hitting six figures - will give us some kind of permanent satisfaction. That if we work hard enough, success will reward us with happiness.

But what they don't tell you is this:

Success without purpose is empty.
It doesn't fill the void; it only magnifies it.

I've had my fair share of socially-accepted wins. I've got a degree, I've made viral videos, I've received countless academic accolades, I've celebrated big sporting achievements, I've spoken on stage in front of thousands of people. From the outside looking in, I have a million reasons to be happy. And yet, every time I've crossed off another achievement, the fulfilment I was expecting never showed up. It's a weird feeling to realise that the thing you've been working towards - sometimes for years - doesn't actually make you feel any different. Instead, you're left chasing the next milestone, hoping maybe that one will finally do it.

Spoiler: it won't.

This chapter isn't about bashing ambition. Ambition is good. Progress is good. But we have to talk about what happens when success becomes your identity. When you start needing every win to prove the last one wasn't a fluke. Because eventually, *you stop aiming for purpose and start running from failure.*

. . .

Ever since I was young, I dreamt of building my own business. Entrepreneurship was something that just made sense to me - choose your own hours, your own salary, your own office, your own life - right? If I was going to spend my life working, I wanted to spend it working for me, not for someone else. But, I also understood that I couldn't just start a business without any real value to offer society. I had to get some experience before anything else.

My first taste of business was watching my mum and step-dad take on the surfing industry. They invented a car seat cover that let surfers drive home wet without ruining the seat; and they called it the Wetpatch. Kinky, right? The Wetpatch was a neoprene car seat cover that went over the headrest and allowed any wet person to sit on it without wetting the seat underneath. It was the perfect venture. An industry they were interested in, a product that was simple, but effective, and a plan to commercialise their success. They broke-even in their first year (a feat that many business owners don't accomplish at all). They had a great product, they put in the hard work, they were receiving great feedback - it looked like a success.

And then, they told me they were going to shut up shop after 2 years in business. Not because they stopped believing in the product, but because the business wasn't right for them. They were still working full-time jobs, they still had a mortgage to pay, they were still stuck in the rat-race and this extra work just wasn't worth it. So, as any 16-year-old would do, I said I'd take over. I 'bought' the company for $1 on the premise I would run the business and they would help me sell the remaining stock. I was the CEO of Wetpatch for about 3 weeks. I presented it in class, I posted about it to my 2,000 Instagram followers, I asked people to buy one - nothing came of it. I gave up. Here I was, this 16-year-old who thought he could take over the world, and I couldn't even sell a handful of car seat covers. The realisation that maybe I wasn't cut out for business hit hard. And it wasn't the failure that stung, it was the hit to my ego. I wasn't the smart, business-savvy kid I thought I was, and that shook me more than I wanted to admit.

. . .

It wasn't until after high school that I decided to act on this deeply ingrained desire of mine once again. I was back at Freshwater Senior Campus, this time not as a student, though. My job was to provide academic support to students who found the classroom a tough place for learning - from trouble at home to diagnosed learning impairments, these students found it incredibly tough to fit the typical school system that they were forced to participate in, especially by the time they reached Year 11 and Year 12 after years of slowly falling behind due to insufficient support systems.

The experience of helping these students was an eye-opening one for me. I had never considered that the starting line wasn't an even one, that some people had to fight harder than me to be successful during high school. So, in my infinite 19-year-old wisdom and despite having done absolutely zero market research, I decided to start a blog. Uncle Nathan was born. My goal with Uncle Nathan was to share what I had learned about 'success in the HSC' with students who may not be privy to the same information, or who were unfortunate enough to not fit the school system. Essentially, I wanted to give them a guide to get good marks without having to somehow go back in time 5 years and listen better in class. This was my second taste of business. I spent $155 on the domain name 'unclenathan.com', built a website with a few blog posts (yes, before

ChatGPT existed - it wasn't easy), and then I launched it to those same Facebook and Instagram friends that I had launched Wetpatch to just a few years earlier.

5,000 website sessions on the first day, 200 Instagram followers, reshares from people I hadn't heard from in months - Uncle Nathan was a success, and I felt great. What's interesting about this whole experience was that I didn't make a single dollar in the first 6 months of Uncle Nathan, and yet, I felt like I had a successful business that fulfilled me. Young people resonated deeply with Uncle Nathan's message. They understood the pain I was trying to address because they had also lived it. They appreciated the sincerity of a 'business' that wasn't trying to make money, but instead, was trying to help people above all else.

I began to realise, though, I had actually just built a passion project, not a business. Nonetheless, Uncle Nathan grew into a huge success. I launched a podcast on Spotify and a TikTok page for marketing, amassing millions of views and tens of thousands of podcast downloads. I was making a real impact, and the numbers were showing it. Then, I built a course to take into high schools. It was an hour-long talk which taught 16-18-year-olds the basics of financial literacy. This was the tool I would use to turn Uncle Nathan into a proper business - and it worked. I booked a few school gigs, a contract with the local council, and some content of the course attracted a few hundred thousand views on TikTok.

Uncle Nathan was making money, it was profitable, and I finally had a successful business. But all of a sudden, I began to feel resentment towards it. I felt like my school talks were uninspiring, I didn't have the same motivation to edit my podcast episodes, I lost sight of my goals, and I didn't know what else I could do to help people. I had just achieved my exact definition of success: get paid to do what I love and helps others; and yet, I felt unfulfilled again. And the scariest part was realising I couldn't blame anyone else for how empty it felt.

The problem was that turning something I loved into a business meant it stopped being something I loved. What once felt like a creative outlet now felt like a job, and not the kind of job I got excited about. It wasn't about helping people anymore - it was about sponsorship deals, school contracts, and making sure my content 'performed.' The pressure to keep growing killed the passion and instead of feeling inspired, I felt burdened. The brand alone had done wonders for me personally, I was picking up guest podcast appearances, invited to speak at conferences with more than 5,000 people in the crowd, even the Daily Mail wrote a couple of articles about my podcast. To be honest, Uncle Nathan was doing more for me than it was for others, and as much I wanted to, I just couldn't figure out how to rebalance that.

Now, I'm sure you're probably wondering why there isn't a 'happy ending' to the story above. Why there is no 'key takeaway' for you to implement into your own life. Truth be told, I haven't actually figured out the next part of this story, yet. I'm writing this book to share the idea that the confusion you are feeling right now in your 20s is not an uncommon experience. You might not have started a business of your own or generated Z-list TikTok virality - but, I can guarantee you have also had a time in the last few years where you've questioned everything you are doing and wondered:

'What is next for me?'

And, that's where I'm at right now as well.

. . .

So, back to the whole 'success is empty' thing. I've already bragged about my achievements in high school, and now my success in the adult world with Uncle Nathan, but, what I haven't told you about is the issue with all of this. The issue was (and still is) - every time I felt success, I felt an immense pressure to replicate it. I have never allowed myself to be proud of my achievements because I've always been so focused on the next one.

DUX of Year 9? Cool, now you've got to do it again.

DUX of Year 10? Great, now you're moving to a new school - good luck, buddy.

No awards in Year 11? You basically failed.

Excelled in Year 12? That's only because you felt so hopeless at last year's awards ceremony.

Finally made the starting team for football? Great, you've worked so hard to get there - now don't fuck it up.

Took a holiday? That wasn't very smart, now you've lost your starting spot and you haven't posted on Uncle Nathan for 5 days.

Video goes viral on Uncle Nathan? Cool, but why did the next one only get 2,000 views?

Podcast in the top 1%? Nice, but why isn't it in the top 0.5%?

With every win, the stakes got higher. It wasn't just about achieving anymore - it was about proving that the last time wasn't a fluke, and I felt that pressure growing with every new success. It's not like people were directly expecting me to keep winning, but I felt like they were. I felt like I had to meet some invisible standard. I wasn't chasing success anymore - I was running from the fear of failure. And every time I crossed off a goal, the pressure to outdo myself only grew.

Psychologists call this the "arrival fallacy" - the illusion that once we achieve a goal, we'll finally be happy. But studies show that our brains adapt quickly to wins, and we're wired to crave the next hit and that's why so many high achievers feel empty after a win...

The truth is, every time we level up we have to face a new challenge - and that's just what comes with a life of progression. I'd say I'm one of the lucky ones because I can actually recognise these thoughts. It wasn't always like this, but now I know I should celebrate my successes, and I'm getting better at doing that. I interviewed a friend of mine, Alex Hayes, on the Uncle Nathan podcast in 2022 and he said something that has brought some clarity to this feeling;

"Another level, another devil"

Success, in terms of 'levelling up' in life, will always come with new challenges to face, new pressures to withstand, new expectations to meet, and it is possible to accept these challenges while allowing yourself to enjoy that moment of success, even if just briefly.

. . .

Now that we've spoken about what comes after 'success,' I want to deeply explore what comes before it. As my passion for Uncle Nathan started to decline, I fell into one of the most exciting opportunities of my life - a chance to move abroad and live in Bali with a girl I'd just met (but liked a lot). There were a couple of major sticking points to figure out:

1. How would I make money?
2. What would I do about uni?

I was working part time for a startup in Sydney (marketing), and was three years through a four-year degree. I decided to quit my job and start a digital marketing agency on the premise that the startup I was working for would become my first client and pay my bills while I build systems and find new clients. I also decided to drop-out of uni. Not drop-out in the typical sense, but I had the opportunity to close that door with 1 degree and 1 diploma instead of doing the extra year to graduate with 2 full degrees - I was okay with that outcome so that's what I did. So much could go wrong, but for me, moving overseas, building a business from scratch, free from uni, living on a tropical island with amazing surf, and building a relationship with a girl I really connected with - now that was a pretty exciting (and scary) next chapter. So, that's what I did. I let Uncle Nathan take a back seat and I focused on my new version of success:

- A profitable business
- A successful relationship
- A deep feeling of happiness in Bali
- A new friendship group to build great memories with
- A frequent and exciting travel routine

I never really stopped to think about why I wanted these things, they sort of just made sense with the new stage I was at. I also didn't think about the opportunity cost of each version of success.

> Economists use the term "opportunity cost" to describe what we give up when we say yes to something else, and studies show this cost often isn't financial, but emotional. Saying yes to one version of life means mourning the one you didn't choose, even if it looks good on paper.

One hard truth I have learned in my 25 years of life is this:

We certainly can have it all, but not all at once.

With everything we choose to do, every goal we choose to go after, every journey we decide to embark on, we are simultaneously choosing to not do something else, to *not* go after a different goal. This is the opportunity cost of each version of success we choose to seek. Like I did back in Year 12, I put my head down and got to work on this new definition of success. I built Finsightful Media (my marketing agency) up to a six-figure agency in a couple of months and was able to pay myself enough to live a pretty nice life in Bali. I was able to dedicate time to building a new relationship with someone who I was growing to care deeply about. This one was super important considering we had just moved across the world to be with each other and were now tasked with the challenge of living together in a new country, with a new language and both of us working online. I know it sounds like a dream, but spending that much time together in a brand new relationship with the stress of work, maintaining a villa (and within a couple of months - a new puppy), could have well and truly sent us both insane.

I had also made some new friends in Bali who I thought were really cool and interesting people. I was being invited to the biggest events on the island with free alcohol and VIP seating every single night of the week if I wanted it. We certainly were turning Bali into our new home. The interesting thing is, only now in writing this am I realising that I actually was doing all of the things I had hoped I would achieve by moving to Bali. It definitely hasn't, until this moment, felt anything like a 'success' in the typical sense of the word, and each of these micro-successes have come at different stages of the journey.

. . .

So, with everything going right in these first few months I decided it would be silly not to continue levelling up. I kept networking, meeting interesting people and making connections. Pretty early on in this whole networking shemozzle, we met some amazing guys who were running a weekly event in Bali. We attended the first Inno at Da Maria and decided this would be our Wednesday night event for the next few weeks. On one of these Wednesday night events I got speaking to another guy from Australia. He'd experienced a pretty similar upbringing to myself, he had moved to Bali around 4 months before I had, and he also ran his own marketing agency. The only facet of digital marketing that his agency didn't specialise in was the exact facet of digital marketing that I had become a little wizkid at - performance marketing (aka Meta and Google ads).

I was intrigued by the proposition to come on board and expand my business into a new market, a market I was now living in. But, at the same time, I was hesitant to give up the business I had just built to be profitable and functioning almost without any of my input at all. It didn't take long for me to commit to the new agency. Within 6 months, I had basically paused Finsightful Media and was working full-time for this new agency with a fully-fledged Indonesian work visa and a piece of the pie. But there was some hesitation. Something didn't feel quite right. The promises were big - ownership, expansion, growth - but I ignored the nagging voice telling me to slow down and think it through. There were red flags, too: the constant turnover, the pressure to work long hours. I brushed them aside, telling myself it was just part of the hustle. After all, this was 'success,' right? I pushed through, thinking I had no choice. But deep down, I knew I was ignoring my gut, and that choice would cost me.

The issue with this situation wasn't that what I was doing was wrong or not working. The issue was that I didn't feel fulfilled or inspired anymore. I had let Uncle Nathan fall off, I had paused my business which I had full ownership and control over and in doing so I had given myself longer hours for lower pay. I had also let my relationship begin to go stale because I was spending so much time working and so little time enjoying the tropical paradise I was living in. I didn't realise it at the time, but I was burning out. Every morning, I woke up with a sinking feeling - like I was trapped in the very life I had spent years working to create. Success, on the outside, looked great, but inside, I was running on fumes.

This disconnect has a name. Researchers call it "surface acting" - when you project success but feel nothing inside. Over time, it can lead to emotional exhaustion, cynicism, and a sense of detachment from your own life.

I had nothing left to give. The pressure, the long hours, the constant hustle - I had become a slave to my own version of success, and it was suffocating me. I didn't allow myself to focus on the one thing that should come before success - purpose. Instead, I focused on the end goal and the perception that I was thriving overseas and levelling up. I had become blind to my own definition of happiness but was too stuck-in-a-rut to notice. The thing is, I thought Bali would bring me everything I'd been working towards - freedom, success, a sense of purpose. In my mind, it was the next big level-up. But what I didn't anticipate was that even on a tropical island, the same pressures and expectations would follow me.

I'll say this again here because it fits...

You absolutely can have everything you want in life, but you won't get it all at once.

...

By now, you've probably realised the same thing I have: success, as we're taught to understand it, is more of a moving target than a final destination.

You can chase milestone after milestone, hit career goals, financial wins, relationship highs, and yet, somehow, you'll still be left wanting more. That's because I don't think true fulfilment is found by achieving the next big thing - it's found by understanding *why* you're chasing it in the first place. I was so focused on ticking off the next box and living up to an unrealistic image of success that I completely lost track of my own purpose.

What was I even working toward?

Was it validation?

Was it pride?

Was it the expectation that once I hit this goal, life would finally feel complete?

I guess life doesn't work like that. Every time I've achieved something big - whether it was launching my first business, making a viral video, or moving across the world - there's always been this nagging emptiness lurking beneath the surface. I hadn't figured out the purpose behind it and I was stuck in this cycle of thinking, "Once I get this, everything will feel right." But it never did. What I've learned, slowly and sometimes painfully, is that success without purpose is just noise. It looks good from the outside, but it doesn't mean anything if it's not aligned with what really matters to you.

And here's the thing: no one else can define your purpose for you. It's not about what society says you should achieve. It's not about what your parents, friends, or social media expects from you. It's about figuring out what makes *you* feel alive, what drives you, what gives you energy when the grind feels never-ending. Unfortunately, I don't have the answer to what your purpose is. I barely know mine most days. But I know what it's not. It's not your job title, your follower count, or how impressed other people are when they hear what you do.

Success without meaning will wear you out. It'll give you a quick hit of dopamine, followed by a slow bleed of emptiness. So yes, chase the goals. Build the business. Post the video. Go after the big thing. But just know this:

The finish line never feels as good as you think it will, unless you know why you're crossing it in the first place.

That's what no one tells us - that clarity won't come after you succeed, it will come after you stop trying to *perform* your life, and start actually living it. This isn't the end of the chapter because I've figured it all out. It's the end because I finally realised I don't have to.

Not so quick...

If something stuck from this chapter, if a belief was challenged, or a certain thought made an impact - this is where you might want to take a second to reflect on it.

Write it down if you want to, or just sit with it for a few seconds.

Is What I Know Actually So?

Complete this sentence:

If I'm being honest, I think I'm chasing __________________ (goal) because I want to feel ____________________ (emotion).

Then, ask yourself:

Could I achieve this feeling without achieving this goal?

Allow yourself to sit with the thought for a second or two - if the answer is no, it may be time to rethink where your validation is coming from...

Chapter 3

WHOSE LIFE IS THIS?

We all do it. Intentional or not, we shape so much of our lives around what other people expect from us. Whether it's family, friends, or society in general, the pressure to live up to someone else's version of success is constant. From a young age, we're told what's "right" and what's "wrong" - get good grades, land a secure job, build a stable life. We're shown a path, a checklist of what success should look like. It's not always spoken aloud, sometimes it's subtle. It's in the way your parents talk about job security or the pride in their voice when you bring home a great exam result. And for a while, it works. You follow the path laid out for you, tick the boxes, and everyone seems happy. But somewhere along the way, you start to feel the weight of it and all of a sudden, you find yourself striving for a version of success you don't even recognise.

For as long as I can remember, I've felt like I had to be better than average. The truth is, I think this way not because I need perfection, but because I've been made to believe I'm capable of it. It's a strange paradox: my own potential has become a source of pressure. If I don't hit perfection, it feels like I'm failing everyone around me, even if no one else would see it that way. And when you finally realise that, it's like a punch to the gut. You start questioning every decision you've made - was this really what I wanted, or was it just what I thought I was supposed to want? Suddenly, the life you've been building starts to feel like it belongs to someone else and you're left wondering: *how did I get here?*

I've been there, I mean, I'm still there sometimes. Trying to meet the expectations of my family, my friends, even the expectations I've set for myself. And I know it's exhausting. It feels like you're running on a treadmill, and no matter how hard you push, you never actually go anywhere. You're constantly striving for approval, constantly working towards some vague idea of "success" that never seems to fully materialise. The irony is, the harder you try to reach that perfection, the further you drift from your own sense of self and the more emotional exhaustion you feel trying to fit into a mould that was never meant for you. The only way to stop feeling this is to learn how to let it go. To figure out what you want, independent of what everyone else thinks you should want, and to start living life on your own terms. Because living under the weight of other people's expectations is a heavy burden to carry - and at some point, we have to decide to set it down.

. . .

Assuming you've actually read and been paying attention to what I've written so far, you'll know that my life as an adolescent and young adult has been quite focused around this notion of 'success' in the typical sense of the word. Success in my personal life, success in my professional life, success in my academic life, and success in my sporting life. The thing about this highly strung notion of success is that nothing I do is ever quite good enough. Well, that's how it feels anyway. And sometimes I have to stop and question that feeling…

Why don't I feel like my achievements are good enough?

Why can I do 99 things right and spend a week thinking about the 1 thing I did wrong?

Why does perfection seem possible even though I know that it's not?

I'm beginning to realise, upon reflection, that I feel this way not necessarily because my success isn't good enough, but because my expectations aren't aligned with the reality of what success actually looks like. The standards I hold myself to are largely shaped by what I assume others expect of me and by society's definition of success. These expectations aren't truly my own.

Whenever I take on a new challenge, my goal is always to be the best because anything less feels like failure. I think this way because deep down, I know I have the potential to excel. Falling short of perfection feels like I'm letting myself down, even if no one else sees it that way. It wasn't about being perfect the very first time, I was happy to put in the work to become the best, but, if I wasn't the best by the time I expected to be the best, I was disappointed and discouraged to continue. If I believed a certain thing about a specific part of my life, and that was ever questioned, I found it incredibly difficult to bounce back. And this belief has been prevalent throughout everything I've done for as long as I can remember...

Growing up, I got used to being told I was good at things. School came easily. Sport did too. I was often "ahead of the curve," or at least that's what I was told. So when I didn't get DUX one year, or got injured just as I was progressing, or experienced rejection for the first time - I didn't see them as isolated moments. I saw them as evidence. Evidence that maybe I wasn't as capable as I'd been led to believe. And instead of bouncing back, I shrank. I pulled away. I stopped trying. Not because I didn't care, but because I cared too much. It's funny, I think back to all of those examples and realise that, had I known about this expectation trap back then, I probably would have pushed through each one and gone on to achieve the thing I let myself stop believing in. But then again, I never would have learned to think in this way if it wasn't for those experiences occurring.

I've found that some of the toughest expectations to deal with aren't always the ones that come from other people. Instead, they're the ones we put on ourselves. My dad was a football coach, but he said I could play rugby if I wanted to, or basketball, or tennis, or cricket, or any other sport under the sun. There was no expectation for me to play the sport he made a living from - and yet, I felt like there was. I enjoyed football, and I had a dad who was great at it, therefore, it made sense for me to want to be the best. But, I also enjoyed basketball and surfing and snowboarding and skating and softball and cricket. I was torn between my love for football and my love for so many other sports. My friends saw me as the kid who was good at everything, my family saw me as the kid who was good at everything and I saw myself as the kid who was good at everything.

Then, I missed out on the cricket team in year 5. I guess there was something I couldn't do. And that one failure rocked my entire world. It wasn't just because I missed out on a spot - it was what I believed that failure said about me that I found difficult to accept. My whole identity was challenged. I'd always seen myself as the kid who could excel at anything I put my mind to. So, if I was meant to be the best, how did I miss out on a team? It was the first time I had to confront the idea that maybe I wasn't as capable as I'd always believed, and that tough realisation hit me harder than the rejection itself. From that point, I began to question my ability more often. Not just in sports, but in everything I did. It planted a seed of doubt that I carried with me into other areas of my life, shaping how I approached challenges moving forward.

I pretended that I didn't care. I told myself:

I didn't make the cricket team, but I didn't really try anyway. I was definitely good enough, I just didn't want to play sports that term...

This is the narrative I wanted people to think. Of course, I wasn't going to let anyone know the truth. I eventually boiled my love for sports down into a top 4 - soccer, snowboarding, basketball, surfing. I loved each one of them and the idea of turning any of those sports into a career was something I found extremely exciting. On any given day, you'd find me fantasising about the life of a professional athlete in any of those 4. With the benefit of hindsight now up my sleeve, it's clear to me that my expectation to be the best didn't line up with the reality of what 'being the best' actually required. If I wanted to be the best soccer player, I would have had to stop training for basketball 3 times a week and playing a game every Saturday, I'd have to stop spending 20-40 days in the snow every year, and I wouldn't be able to keep attending surf training on a Wednesday afternoon. If I truly wanted to be the best soccer player, I should have been training 4-5 days each week and playing at the top level for my age group. As you can see, my expectations and my reality were far from aligned.

I guess it's pretty obvious looking back that I was never going to make it in any of these sports unless I dedicated myself to just one. But, I didn't want to choose just one. I loved it all and I wanted it all. Nonetheless, I let my expectations dictate my confidence in these things and in the rest of my life without understanding the reality of those expectations. I felt my goals slipping away quickly and I thought it was because I wasn't good enough to be the best. But, that's not true. I was good enough. We are all good enough to do whatever it is we want to do. It just comes down to how much work we're willing to put in. Our expectations should be aligned with our situation. For example, if we expect to be the top 1%, we should act like the top 1%. If I expected to be in the top 1% of soccer players, I needed to train harder than the other 99% of soccer players. In truth, I was nowhere near that level - but, it took me a long time to see that.

. . .

So, in some ways I've learned to tame the expectation trap and prevent my own unrealistic expectations from bringing my confidence down. But, in many other ways I still let this affect me in daily life. When I decided to move to Bali, I was buzzing with excitement. I knew this was a huge step for me, something that could reshape my entire life. It was an adventure I craved - a chance to grow, make new friends, and take on challenges I hadn't faced before. But alongside the excitement, there was something else: this sense of validation. I knew that people back home would see this move as a bold, crazy achievement, and to be honest, that made me feel proud. The thought of others talking about 'Nathan - the guy who moved to Bali and started his own business' was intoxicating. It wasn't just about the move itself; it was about what the move represented. There was a kind of validation wrapped up in the idea of stepping into this new identity. I felt like I was finally living up to the expectations other people had for me - and, in a way, the expectations I had for myself. It felt like I had 'made it,' at least in the eyes of everyone watching from the outside. The thread I assumed everyone was talking about went something like this:

"I knew Nath would do something awesome one day. He always had that drive to do something different."

It was true. I'd done what everyone expected of me. I did something that most people wouldn't do. I took a risk and enabled a life that many dream of, but rarely make happen. The first few months were filled with people replying to stories and posts expressing how proud they were of the move I'd made. I craved this sort of attention. I wanted everyone around me to validate the decision I had made by making me feel like I was better than most - I was the best. Pretty quickly, however, this turned into a strong inner conflict. I'd just levelled up, everyone was impressed, but, there was now a new expectation to level up again. The replies began to slow as my friends and followers got used to my new reality. It didn't seem as impressive anymore because it wasn't new. The expectation became - 'what's next for Nathan?'

Whether anyone even thought this or not, didn't matter. This is what I thought people were thinking, and therefore, it became my expectation for myself. This was a problem because I began to feel like I wasn't levelling up anymore.

I was in a stable relationship.

I had a beautiful villa to live in.

I had found new and exciting work.

I was earning more money than before.

I found a new group of cool friends.

And yet, I was actually feeling unhappy despite living the life I had dreamt of for so long.

Psychology research actually backs this up:

> People who fixate on external markers of success (like status or approval) tend to report more anxiety and lower life satisfaction, whereas those who focus on their own inner goals (personal growth, relationships) have much better well-being.

I had let this expectation of levelling up cloud my gratitude for the level I was at. I had convinced myself that because I wasn't outwardly showing my new levels, I was in fact, stagnating. Writing this chapter whilst in that exact position has brought a sense of clarity to the situation. The truth is, I am still levelling up. My life in Bali is a good one, I have healed through significant loss and heartache, I have taken big risks to follow my passions, I am learning a new language. There are so many parts of my life that are still evolving, I just don't share them on social media like I used to and therefore, I don't get the external validation that I became so reliant on.

Every day, I'm learning to recalibrate my expectations and realign them with what truly matters to me. I'm starting to live in a way that brings me genuine happiness - not because it checks off someone else's boxes, but because I'm choosing to focus on what feels right for me. I've realised that my fulfilment doesn't need to be tied to meeting anyone else's standards. Instead, it's about doing good for others while also honouring myself. That's where real success lies - not in external validation, but in living authentically, on my own terms. I understand now that I won't ever really know what people think of me and what they expect me to achieve, and I've realised that any attempt to figure that out or let that dictate what I expect of myself will only ever lead to disappointment. As long as I am striving for validation of every milestone, I will never feel like I have accomplished anything because there will always be another level to obtain. Levelling up should come from a place of desire to learn something new rather than a need to actualise what's expected of me from others.

...

At the end of the day, living under the weight of other people's expectations - whether real or imagined - will drain you. It's a game you can never win, because the rules keep changing. As soon as you meet one standard, another appears, and then another. You find yourself constantly chasing validation and realise that it feels as fleeting as it does unsatisfying. The truth is, no matter how much approval you get from others, it will never be enough to fill the void that comes from ignoring what you actually want. The hardest part about this realisation is that it doesn't come all at once. It sneaks up on you over time, little by little, until one day we're in our mid 30s wondering how we got there. You start to question whether the decisions you've made are really yours, or if they've been influenced by what you thought you were supposed to do. And in that moment, the weight of other people's expectations hits you like a ton of bricks. But that's also the moment when you have a choice - to keep carrying that weight, or to finally set it down.

I've started to see that the expectations I've placed on myself - whether because of societal pressure, family influence, or my own internal drive - haven't always been aligned with what truly makes me happy. I've spent years chasing perfection, chasing "success" as it's been defined for me by others, and constantly measuring myself against an impossible standard. But I'm learning that success doesn't have to look like what we've been told. It doesn't have to mean being the best at everything, or hitting certain milestones by a certain age. The reality is, the only expectations that matter are the ones that align with your own values and your own version of success. Letting go of those external expectations doesn't mean giving up on ambition or not striving for more. It means redefining what "more" looks like for you. It's about focusing on the things that bring you fulfilment, not just the things that look good on paper or impress other people. And it's about trusting yourself enough to know that your path doesn't have to look like anyone else's, and that's okay. So, if there's one thing I've learned from all this, it's that despite how cliché it sounds, life really is too short to live by someone else's playbook. The weight of those expectations will crush you if you let them. But once you decide to live on your own terms - when you start aligning your actions with your own sense of purpose - that's when you'll finally feel the freedom you've been searching for.

Not so quick...

If something stuck from this chapter, if a belief was challenged, or a certain thought made an impact - this is where you might want to take a second to reflect on it.

Write it down if you want to, or just sit with it for a few seconds.

Is What I Know Actually So?

Think back to a standout moment when someone praised you - a teacher, a parent, a coach.

Now, complete this sentence:

That moment made me think I had to continue to be ____________ to be worthy.

Then, ask yourself:

Does that belief still serve me, or have I just never stopped to question it?

You might be surprised by what comes to mind.

Part 2

WHEN CLARITY FEELS LIKE A MYTH

Chapter 4

TOO MANY DOORS

In the world I've grown up in, I have undoubtedly been conditioned to believe that *more options = more freedom.* With endless possibilities at our fingertips, it feels like we should be able to craft the perfect life, handpick the ideal career, and build a flawless relationship. Which all sounds incredible in theory, right? We're made to feel that the sheer number of choices we have is empowering, that it's a privilege our generation is lucky to have; and please don't get me wrong, it absolutely is a privilege to have choices. But, what no one really talks about is how overwhelming that kind of freedom can be. Having choices doesn't always make things easier. It can leave us stuck, paralysed by indecision, and afraid that we might make the wrong move. It's funny how something as simple as making a decision can turn into such a stressful experience. You'd think that having more options would bring a feeling of liberation, but instead, I've found more often than not it does the opposite.

And the longer you stand there, the harder it gets to make a move. You start worrying that if you choose one path, you'll miss out on what may have been down the other paths. So, naturally, the fear of making the wrong decision becomes so strong that you end up making no decision at all. I've been there more times than I care to admit - paralysed by too many choices, unable to decide which direction to take. Whether it was choosing between different career paths, deciding on a new business venture, or even figuring out what to do in my personal life, I've felt the weight of indecision. And in those moments, I realised something important: waiting for the perfect path to show itself is the trap. It's easy to get caught up in the idea that there's one right answer, but the truth is, no matter what you choose, you'll never know for sure if it was the "right" decision until you've lived through it.

This chapter is about that feeling - being paralysed by too many options and the pressure to make the perfect choice. It's about the mental toll of overthinking and the realisation that sometimes, the best thing you can do is just start moving, even if you're not sure where it'll lead. Because in the end, making a decision in the name of growth, even if it's imperfect, will forever outweigh the consequences of choosing to remain the same.

. . .

I often catch myself thinking about what life might have been like 100 years ago. There was no social media, travel was expensive and technology was much less advanced. A person's life was significantly predetermined by where they were born, what their parents did for a living, and what they were taught - that was it. People back then knew what they knew, and were relatively oblivious to what they didn't know. There were no Instagram accounts flaunting immense wealth and no YouTube gurus selling a course to millions. If your parents believed in a good education, that's what you'd get - no questions asked. If you learnt a trade, you stuck to it for life. Taking a gap year to travel the world wasn't a thing - or if it was, it was only for the mega-rich. And then, along came technology.

2.5 billion gigabytes of content are produced online every 24 hours.

To give you some perspective, that's enough data to fill 12.5 million MacBooks, produced every single day! Young people today quite literally have millions of hours of content readily accessible to them at any given second. We also have the ability to travel thousands of kilometres with a single YouTube video or a relatively cheap plane ticket if you want the authentic experience. We are privy to any and all information that has ever existed. If we wanted to, we could learn just about anything, regardless of where we were born, who our parents are and how much money we have. In what world could anyone who lived 100 years ago fathom this kind of flexibility and freedom? And this undeniable liberty that we are privileged to accept as everyday life truly can be such a powerful motivator; but, at the same time it can also be the sole inhibitor of happiness and true progress.

This paradox made the end of high school incredibly tough for me. In our younger years, we're encouraged to more or less pick one thing - one career path, one passion, one goal. The typical question: 'what do you want to be when you grow up?' always had the expectation of a two word answer:

'A ______'

'A *doctor*'

'A *lawyer*'

'A *policeman*'

'An *astronaut*'

'A *nurse*'

'An *actor*'

This is how most of us think when we are young. My first answer to this question was 'An athlete.' More specifically, I wanted to be a professional soccer player. And that would be my dream from the age of 6 to 11. I loved playing soccer and I loved the idea of being famous. It made logical sense. My next answer to that question was 'A lawyer' - this one stuck from the age of 12 to 15 and I was pretty adamant that this would be a good career for me. Soccer became less enjoyable and my career motivation shifted to become purely monetary. I was excited about the idea of wearing a suit to work every day and making great money, but I quickly realised how much reading was involved in being a lawyer and decided that wasn't for me either. In line with the 'rich man' suit obsession, my third answer to that question was 'An investment banker' - the answer that carried the most conviction and certainty out of all three. This one stuck with me from the age of 16 to 19 and still, I was motivated by the idea of making millions and feeling important because I was wearing a suit every day.

At the age of 16, I fell in love with the financial markets. I obsessed over movies like 'The Wolf of Wall Street' and 'The Big Short,' and would spend hours in my bedroom after school studying the concept of investing and the stock market. I learned that there were many different ways to be involved in finance. Did I want to become a day trader, or should I be a stock broker? Or, maybe I'll stick to fundamental analysis and just invest in great companies over a long-term time horizon like Warren Buffett? The deeper I dug, the more I realised how much I didn't know and how many choices I had to make. I watched a few YouTube videos and decided this would be the thing I'd devote my life to understanding. I didn't exactly know why I found it so fascinating, but my desire to build wealth at the ripe old age of 16 was incredibly strong. A few friends took an interest in what I was doing but no one was interested enough to do it with me. I started investing with fake money to try my luck in the markets and again, other kids were curious but they just thought I was some kind of genius and it was out of reach for them. This behaviour massively inflated my ego and made me think I actually knew what I was doing. Oh, how much I still didn't know…

As I've grown through my 20s, I've become a firm believer in the philosophy of 'the one thing.' It's the idea that true greatness comes from dedicating yourself fully to a single pursuit, rather than spreading your energy across one hundred different things at the same time. When I was 16, I genuinely found that one thing in the financial markets - I had a burning passion and a clear focus. But as life got louder and the distractions piled up, I let the noise drown out that clarity. It's something I still struggle with today. I was primed to make a lot of money at a young age in the financial markets. I had a burning desire, I was tech savvy, I was smart, hell I even looked at investing in Bitcoin in 2018. Also, I actually put in the hours - sometimes up to six hours a day after school - which is a lot for a 16 year old kid who should probably be playing video games instead.

But then, as life began to get inevitably chaotic and increasingly stressful into my late teens, I quickly lost that clarity. With high school coming to an end, I had to study for my exams, think about university, train for soccer, get my licence, maintain a social life, enjoy my dating era… the point is, there was so much more to think about than simply: wake up, go to school, come home and learn about the markets, go to sleep, repeat. I had so many choices in front of me now that it was no longer a matter of one thing, but instead turned into everything all at once.

At 25 years old now, I look back in hindsight with a mix of nostalgia and regret. It's easy to say that I'm happy with where I've ended up, but I'd be lying if I said I didn't have doubts. There's a part of me that aches when I think about the paths I didn't take. What if I had doubled down on the financial markets when I first got curious? What if I hadn't let the fear of missing out pull me in so many directions? It's frustrating because I know deep down that I've wasted time chasing ideas that weren't even mine to begin with. I let social media and the people around me convince me that I needed to follow the mainstream career path. Even though I was entrepreneurial, I had convinced myself that I needed to go to uni to get a degree and work my way up the corporate ladder.

The tossing and turning that went on in my mind during the ages of 17, 18 and 19 was exhausting. I bounced between dreams like a kid in a candy store. One week, I wanted the corporate life - investment banking and the security of a 9-5. Then the next, I'd be picturing myself as an entrepreneur with a business empire. I thought about writing a best-selling book, becoming an influencer, travelling the world as a pro athlete, or even ending up on a Hollywood set, but I was so overwhelmed by all of these possibilities that I couldn't commit to any of them. And, instead of excitement and progression, I felt paralysed.

Turns out there's actually a name for this existential angst.

FOBO: the Fear of a Better Option.

It's like FOMO but less cliché. Instead of just fearing you'll miss out, FOBO makes you constantly suspect there's always a better choice out there, which often leads to total indecision and results in us never committing to anything at all.

Social media had become my window into a thousand different lives. Every day, I was being fed a new version of success - a different dream to chase and another reason to let FOBO win. I saw people living incredible lives: the entrepreneur with a successful business, the backpacker exploring new countries, the athlete training for olympic gold. Each life looked amazing, and I felt like I was supposed to want them all, but the truth is, it left me feeling confused and frustrated because I had no idea how to make a choice or how to know if that choice would even be the right one. I wanted it all but I didn't want to compromise on any of it.

Fast forward 5 years and life now, whilst I understand the concept I've just rattled on about, is still just as confusing and hard to navigate. I now have a degree and a pretty strong idea of who I want to be and what I want to do, and yet, it feels like there are more decisions to make now than ever before. I look around and see friends doing all kinds of things - living in Greece, working in the city, backpacking the world, saving lives, making insane money online, adopting puppies in Bali, buying apartments, getting married. It's overwhelming to see so many different paths and I'm constantly wondering: should I be doing that too? Am I missing out on something better?

And not only are we trying to make these massive, life-shaping decisions, but we're also making hundreds of smaller ones every single day. If we genuinely stopped to weigh every option, every outcome, every what-if, we wouldn't function. We'd never leave the house. So instead, our brains look for shortcuts. And that's where our habits are formed.

Habits aren't about discipline or willpower. They're simply a survival mechanism.

Research shows that a huge portion of our daily behaviour is automatic, not conscious. One study published in the *European Journal of Social Psychology* found that up to 40–45% of our daily actions are driven by habit, not active decision-making. In other words, your brain is constantly trying to conserve energy by turning repeated choices into routines.

That's helpful - until it isn't. Because the same system that saves us from decision fatigue can also trap us in patterns we never consciously chose. We default to what's familiar, what's comfortable, what's easy, even when it no longer serves us. And over time, those tiny, automatic choices quietly shape the direction of our lives far more than the big, dramatic decisions we stress over. That's the uncomfortable truth: most of life isn't built by that massive decision you make once every few years, it's built by the small ones you make every day on repeat. So when everything starts to feel overwhelming, when it feels like you're stuck in the same loop, it's worth zooming out. Not to judge yourself, but to notice. To ask which habits are carrying you forward, and which ones are just helping you avoid the discomfort of choosing something new. Because sometimes the reason you feel stuck isn't that you're making the wrong big decisions, it's that your small ones are keeping you exactly where you are.

. . .

I promise the point of this chapter was not to overwhelm you, even though that's probably what it has done so far. The point of this chapter was to remind you that there will always be a thousand what-ifs and a million reasons to not make a decision - and yet, it's exactly this reasoning that you should use as fuel to make every decision, and to make it fast. I believe that our fate is not set, our future is never certain, and blocking out the noise to focus on the few things that are truly important is the easiest way to be happy. So, let's aim to do that. Let's aim to go after what we want whilst appreciating that there will be distractions and diversions. But, as best we can, let's make a conscious effort to say no to short term temptations and find the discipline to keep doing what we think we should be doing. The easiest way to feel like you're not doing enough is to spread yourself too thin, listen to too many opinions, and take on too many responsibilities when you don't need to.

The key to reducing this overwhelming paralysis is to say *NO*. It really is that simple. Say 'no' to things that don't serve your vision, and unapologetically say 'yes' to the things that do. In the beginning, it's okay to be all over the place. You need to taste a little bit of everything before you can figure out what you actually like. But once you find that thing - the one that lights a fire in you - you have to start saying no to everything else. Trust me, I know this is the hard part. We live in a world that tells us we can do it all, but if you want to truly master something, you need to get comfortable with the fact that you'll be missing out on other things in pursuit of that mastery. It's not about spreading yourself thin forever; it's about experimenting until you know what's worth your full focus. When you find that one thing, dial down the complexity. Life should be a combination of hard work rewarded with pleasure. This is my opinion on everything.

Work hard professionally, then treat yourself to a holiday to re-ignite the hunger.

Work hard on your relationship, then treat yourself to a bit of fun to keep the spark alive.

Work hard on your friendships, then treat yourself to some alone time to recharge the battery.

Work hard on your body, then treat yourself to a rest day to allow time to recover.

In all areas of life, balance should be the key, and as soon as you realise where the hard work should be done, you'll understand where the pleasure can be afforded. The goal then becomes to simplify this down to such a formula that there are only ever a few possible paths that you truly desire, and an acceptance that those paths will require sacrifices. Maybe your one thing is the gym, and that means you're too tired after work and your gym session to try that side hustle idea you've been seeing your unemployed friend post about on social media - that's okay, you chose to reward yourself with rest after a long day of hard work - don't let misplaced FOMO ruin the progress you made. Or maybe you stayed back at the office today to get a big presentation finished and you won't be home in time to cook dinner - that's okay, order dinner in, you deserve it - don't let the guilt of not cooking outweigh the benefit of saving yourself from extra work and stress tomorrow.

Our ability to think freely can be a catalyst for positive change when change is needed, but should also be understood and suppressed when it has the potential to take us away from the things that truly make us happy.

It's a constant battle to tame this beast and despite talking like I know exactly how to tame it, I'm nowhere close to figuring out my one thing. Life for me is, and I think always will be, a fight between what I know I should do and what I decide to do in the moment. And the reason I made this chapter so damn confusing is to remind you that life simply is confusing and there will always be another decision to make, another thing to say yes to and another thing to say no to.

. . .

Here's the hard truth about having too many choices:
It feels like freedom, but it often ends up as a prison of indecision.

We're constantly bombarded with new opportunities, paths, and lifestyles, and it's easy to get lost in the noise. We start to believe that we're missing out if we don't explore every single option. We're told we can have it all, but the reality is, chasing every possibility leaves us spread too thin, exhausted, and unable to truly enjoy any of it. I've learned (and am still learning) that life doesn't have to be about maximising every single choice. Instead, it's about making decisions that align with what truly matters to you. It's not about picking the "perfect" option, because that doesn't exist. Every choice you make is going to come with trade-offs, and every path you choose is going to leave other paths unexplored. But that's okay. That's not failure; that's just life. The fear of missing out is a strong motivator, but it's also a liar. It tells you that if you don't seize every opportunity, you'll fall behind. It convinces you that someone else out there is living a better life because they made a different choice. But the truth is, the people who seem the most content aren't the ones who are doing everything, they're the ones who've figured out what they truly want and are pursuing that with unwavering focus and intention.

It took me a long time to realise this, and honestly, I'm still figuring it out. There are days when I'm caught up in the whirlwind of possibilities, second-guessing every decision, wondering if I should be doing more. But what I've come to understand is that clarity doesn't come from weighing every option indefinitely; it comes from action. It comes from making a choice, committing to it, and seeing where it leads. Because even if it turns out to be the "wrong" choice, it's still a step in the right direction, a step closer to figuring out what you truly want (or what you absolutely don't want). There's a strange sense of relief that comes when you finally decide to stop agonising over every little choice and simply commit to a direction. You might not have all the answers, and you might not even know if it's the "right" path, but that's the point - you don't have to. The beauty of life lies within its unpredictability. It's in the unexpected twists and turns that teach you more about yourself than any amount of careful planning ever could.

So, if you're feeling paralysed by too many choices - *take a deep breath...*

Give yourself permission to pick one thing and let go of the rest, at least for now. Trust that you're not making a permanent decision, you're just choosing to move forward. The worst thing you can do is stand still, caught in the illusion that there's a perfect choice waiting to be found. Progress comes from movement, even if it's imperfect. The reality is, no matter which path you take, you'll end up missing out on something. But that's not a loss, it's just part of the process. The goal shouldn't be to experience everything all at once; it should be to experience the things that truly matter to you in a timeline that allows for maximum enjoyment. And the key? Learning to quiet the noise, focus on what you love, and be okay with the fact that you can't do it all. Because in the end, true freedom comes not from having endless choices but from making peace with the ones you've made. And when you do that, you start to realise that the path you're on is exactly where you're meant to be.

Not so quick...

If something stuck from this chapter, if a belief was challenged, or a certain thought made an impact - this is where you might want to take a second to reflect on it.

Write it down if you want to, or just sit with it for a few seconds.

Is What I Know Actually So?

Think about a decision you've been avoiding - the one you keep waiting to feel 100% certain about.

Now, finish this sentence:

I'm waiting to decide because I ________________________________.

Then, ask yourself:

Has waiting made the decision clearer or just heavier?

If your answer to that question is "heavier," it's probably time to just rip that bandaid off...

Chapter 5

LET IT BREAK YOU

I used to think loss was something that happened to other people. Until it happened to me.

Loss is one of the few experiences in life that is guaranteed, yet we're never really prepared for it. You never really get used to it either, no matter how many times you go through it. Whether it's the death of someone we love, the end of a relationship, losing a pet, or watching a lifelong dream slip away, loss has a way of shaking us to our core. It hurts in a way that feels impossible to describe, because it's not only the person or the thing that's gone, it's the future you thought you'd have with them. The routines. The quiet moments. The version of yourself that existed when they were there. It's the way it forces you to confront parts of yourself you'd rather ignore. It's the way it lingers in the quiet moments, catching you off guard when you think you're finally okay. Loss doesn't just take something from you - it changes you. It demands that you grow, even if it feels like you're being dragged through the mud to get there.

What makes loss so devastating is its permanence. It's the realisation that there's no going back, no undoing what's been done. You're left to navigate a new reality that feels foreign and unsteady, a life reshaped by the absence of what once anchored you. It hurts in ways you didn't think were possible, breaking you open and forcing you to feel everything all at once - the pain, the love, the regret, the longing. Loss is messy and unfair, and it doesn't come with a guidebook.

I used to think of loss as something to "get over." As if it were this obstacle that you could power through with enough time and distractions. Unfortunately, what I've learned is that you don't *really* get over a big loss. You simply learn to live alongside it. You find ways to carry it with you, even as you try to move forward. And in the process, you realise that while the grief is excruciating, it's also clarifying. It forces you to strip away the superficial and confront what no longer aligns. But, here's the paradox: while loss has the power to shatter you, it also has the power to shape you. In the aftermath, when the world feels quieter and emptier, there's a strange clarity that starts to emerge. You begin to see what truly matters - not in a vague, inspirational quote kind of way, but in a raw, gut-wrenching way. Things you once thought were important start to fade, and you're left with an unfiltered view of your priorities, your values, and yourself.

In this chapter, I want to talk about that duality - the pain and the growth. I want to share what it felt like to lose some of the most important parts of my life, and how those moments, as devastating as they were, became pivotal turning points for my future. Because while loss is something none of us can escape, it's also where we can find the deepest lessons about ourselves, our relationships, and what we value most. I'm not going to tell you that loss gets easier or that it all happens for a reason, because sometimes I'm not so sure it does. But, I will tell you that loss has a way of revealing truths we'd never have seen otherwise. It will break you, but it will also present the space for you to rebuild. And in those broken pieces, there's an opportunity to create something new - something stronger, something even more meaningful and beautiful.

. . .

Loss doesn't care who you are, what you've built, or how strong you think you are - it just comes. Sometimes, it's like a wrecking ball, sudden and brutal, leaving nothing but rubble where your life used to stand. Other times, it's a slow, creeping shadow you see in the distance, knowing it's heading straight for you, yet powerless to stop it. Either way, it takes something from you, and you're never quite the same afterward.

Just a couple of months after moving to Bali, a little puppy came into my life - Luna. Luna was special. And I know any dog owner would tell you that their dog was special... but my god, the way I loved this dog was unlike anything I could ever express in words. To go from someone who liked dogs but was never really a proclaimed 'dog person', to adopting a 6-week old puppy who was found in a pile of trash on the streets of Kuta, felt like a jump I would never make - and yet, it was the single most impactful decision of my life so far.

When I lost Luna, it hit harder than I had ever experienced. One moment, she was healthy and full of life, chasing after whatever imaginary enemy she thought was lurking in the rice fields. The next, those same rice fields took her from us. Just like that. No warning, no time to prepare myself. In the blink of an eye, my world went from perfect to unrecognisable. Bali didn't just feel different; it felt wrong, like a piece of my love for the place I lived had been ripped out. Like a piece of *me* had been ripped out.

And here's the part that really messes with me... I've lost family members before. People I loved and cared about, people I knew I'd lose eventually because they were sick or getting older. It wasn't easy, but I had time to process it. I knew it was coming, and in some twisted way, that made it manageable. But Luna? She was healthy. She was just a baby. And then she wasn't. It doesn't make sense, and it probably never will.

> The body actually reacts to sudden loss like trauma - known as acute grief. Your chest tightens. Your thoughts blur. Your heart races. It feels like danger, even though there's nothing to fight. That's why it felt like my entire world had been blown up in an instant... because my body genuinely thought it had.

The truth is, loss doesn't have to make sense. It doesn't have to be fair. And when you're in it, nothing anyone says really helps.

"She had a great life and was so lucky to have you two," people told me. "At least you have the memories."

But all I could think was, *I don't want the memories. I want Luna.*

Grief expert David Kessler says what grieving people need most isn't solutions; it's presence. Not silver linings or advice. Just someone willing to sit in it with you. Platitudes often feel hollow not because people mean badly, but because they bypass the reality of the pain.

Actually, a psychiatrist named Jamie Anderson once wrote: "Grief is just love with nowhere to go." And I think that's why no words can fill the hole, because what's missing isn't language, it's love.

. . .

And to top it all off, Luna wasn't the only one we lost. Nine months later, we had to say goodbye to another beautiful puppy - Olive Bean. She was just ten months old. I still don't really know how to talk about it without my throat tightening up. The love I had for my dogs was unlike any love I'd ever experienced. I cannot wait to feel that love again one day. And if you've never raised your own pet, maybe this grief won't make any sense to you. I get it, but I hope you can find the message in this chapter through your own experience. I can't explain what it feels like to lose two dogs in under a year. I don't even think I've fully processed it yet. You tell yourself it's not going to happen again, because surely the universe couldn't be that *cruel.* And then it does. And somehow it hurts even more the second time, I guess because you know how hard it's going to hit.

We found Olive a few weeks before Luna passed. She had been dumped outside a dog shelter in a cardboard box with her sisters - tiny, underweight, scared. We responded to a post from the shelter asking for help. It was only meant to be a foster arrangement. A way to do something kind while we searched for her forever home. We picked the shy one. Cute orange-ish fur, wide eyes, looked a little like a mouse. She clung to us straight away. We named her Olive. At first, Luna's memory made it hard. Everything Olive did reminded us of what we lost. But slowly, she became her own little light. She was playful, gentle, endlessly affectionate. She had this thing where she'd lick every person she met, not just once, but over and over like she was trying to make sure they really felt loved. And that's what she gave us - love. Pure, uncomplicated love. The kind that comes without expectations or conditions. The kind that doesn't ask for anything in return but a scratch behind the ears and a safe place to sleep.

We officially adopted her not long after Luna passed away. Threw her a little party with a dog cake and balloons. Took her on our weekend getaways. Talked about training her, travelling with her, moving her to Australia. She wasn't just a foster puppy anymore. She was ours. Family. Just like Luna was. And then she started coughing. At first, we didn't think much of it. Took her to a local vet. They said it was just a minor infection, gave us some meds and told us not to worry. But something felt off. She kept coughing. She stopped eating. Her energy disappeared. We were in Thailand for a work trip when a friend - who also adopted Olive's biological sister - was looking after her. She noticed that Olive went downhill again overnight and took her back to the vet. They admitted her into the ICU, but we still had no answers. Finally we got home, rushed straight to the vet and saw Olive. And we knew it wasn't just a cough. Something was really wrong. A second opinion confirmed it. The new vet suspected pneumonia at first, which was scary but treatable. But when they did more scans, they found masses. The words came out clunky and half-translated, but the message landed clear: "We are not sure if this is cancer... but we are concerned."

I felt like the air had been sucked out of the room. One moment she was a happy, healthy puppy. The next, we were being told she might have terminal cancer before her first birthday. We did everything we could.

Spent hundreds on tests, drips, medication, supplements, anything that might give her a fighting chance. We visited her every morning and night, kissed her on the head, told her we loved her over and over again. She wagged her tail every time she saw us. She was so strong. But her little body couldn't keep up. She stopped eating. She grew weak and thin. She couldn't lay down without pain, so instead, she'd fall asleep standing up.

Eventually, we made the incredibly painful decision to end her suffering. We took her home from the vet for one last day. We let her sit in the sun. Breathe fresh air. Walk on the sand. We invited her favourite people over to say goodbye. She was calm. Gentle. Present. Like she knew. And then, out of nowhere, the next morning she bounced back. She ate. She wanted to play. Her eyes looked brighter. She licked our hands like she always had. Just one hour before we were set to put Olive to sleep, the vet saw a video of Olive and said "Maybe we should postpone. Maybe it's not cancer." And you know what? We believed it. Of course we did. Because that's what hope does - it tricks you into thinking the impossible might still happen. It gives you this tiny sliver of *maybe*.

So, the next day I left for a once-in-a-lifetime surf trip with Dad. Something we'd been planning for months and dreaming of our whole lives. The timing wasn't great by any means, but now at least I could leave with some hope. I said my goodbyes to Olive, hugged her tight, kissed her face over and over and said, "I'll see you in five days, Bean. Hold on for me."

She couldn't.

The very next day, she crashed again. The vet confirmed her liver was failing. Her organs were shutting down. She was in pain. She was suffering. And we couldn't justify asking her to fight anymore just because we weren't ready to let go. The hardest part? I wasn't there and I couldn't get there in time even if I wanted to. I got a FaceTime call from the vet. I watched Olive take her last breath through a screen. I saw the moment the light left her eyes. I'll never forget that image. Olive was hugged, kissed, and told she was the best girl in the world. And just like that, she was gone.

When I got home from that trip - a trip that somehow held some of the best memories of my life, even while the worst thing was happening - I saw Olive's ashes sitting next to Luna's in our kitchen. And I broke down again. Two urns. Two names. Two souls we loved with everything we had. And I'm still not done grieving. I don't think I ever will be, I'll just keep learning how to live with it.

> Psychologists call this idea *continuing bonds* - the sense that grief never really ends, it just changes form. Dr. Dennis Klass, who coined the term, found that many grieving people report feeling their loved one's presence long after they're gone. And I get that. Even now, I look for any sign I can find that Luna is still in the rice fields, or that Olive is still sleeping peacefully at the end of my bed.

But if Luna taught me about sudden, senseless loss, Olive taught me about the slow kind. The kind where you do everything you can and it still isn't enough. Where you watch someone you love suffer and you can't fix it. You just have to be there. Hold their hand. Kiss their head. Let them go. See, there's something sacred in knowing it's the end. If you know someone's time is limited, everything changes. Every hug feels longer. Every morning matters. You hold them tighter. You love them harder. You actually say the things you want to say. You don't wait. You don't assume you'll have more time. And I realised - maybe we should live like this every day. Because the truth is, we never really know when our last moment with someone will come. That last hug. That last walk. That last dinner. That last breath.

As heartbreaking as it all was, Olive's death felt a little less shocking than Luna's. Not easier, just... different. Maybe I was more prepared. Maybe the trauma of Luna's death had already broken me open. Or maybe I'd just learned how to carry grief better the second time around. Either way, I was reminded again that *nothing is permanent.* No matter how much you love something, it can be taken away from you in an instant. And that's why love matters so much... Because if we don't let ourselves love deeply, sure, we'll never feel the full ache of loss - but, we'll never feel the full joy of love either.

. . .

Grief doesn't care what form it takes. The loss of a life, a relationship, a dream - they all leave the same kind of hollow space. I felt this same confusion when my first long-term, adult relationship ended. It was three years of my life, three years of building this version of the future with someone else, and then it was over. No matter how mutual or "for the best" it was, the breakup left me feeling hollow. Like I'd lost not just the person, but the future I thought we were heading toward. The plans we made together. The version of myself I was when I was with them. I genuinely struggled to see a better future without them in it, and yet, without that happening, I never would've met Luna and Olive or gone on to experience everything I have experienced since. I still think about all of these significant losses, and the thing is, it doesn't get easier. Each one is different, and each one hurts in its own way. But what I've started to realise is that loss isn't just something you go through; it's something you carry. It becomes part of you. It shapes the way you see the world and the way you value the things you still have. I don't believe that everything happens for a reason. But I do believe meaning can be made from everything that happens. Loss doesn't justify itself. It doesn't explain itself. But it does force you to ask better questions. Who matters? What matters? And what am I willing to risk losing again, knowing how much it could hurt?

. . .

The Shared Weight of Loss

Loss is deeply personal, but it's also universal. Every human experiences it, and yet, when we're in it, it feels isolating - like no one else in the world could possibly understand what we're going through. But the truth is, they do. Loss is a language we all end up speaking at some point. And in reading through some of the stories people shared with me, I realised just how much grief connects us, even when it feels like it's tearing us apart. For example, a friend of mine put words to a feeling I had been trying to describe for weeks:

> ***"My experience with loss is one of numbness. It feels like the world stops spinning. Like everyone else should stop what***

they're doing because life as we know it will never be the same again, and yet, no one does. Life continues as it always has been, and I'm the only one grieving."

The truth is, this has been the hardest chapter for me to write. I know what I am trying to say with this chapter but I struggle to find the exact words to do this feeling justice, and it's rare that I can't find words to describe what I'm thinking, but I guess that expresses how deeply confusing loss can be for all of us. So, I want to do something a little different with the end of this chapter. I want to share what loss means to *you*, not just what it means to me. Despite it being a universal experience, everyone deals with loss in their own way. For some, it can take years to get over a devastating moment, and for others, it's easier to compartmentalise and continue with their daily lives. I couldn't really grasp the full extent of grief until I was actually living that shared experience, and now, with those scars, I can truly understand the depths we all fall to in those moments of heartache and confusion.

. . .

The most visceral recount of this feeling came from someone incredibly close to me, and it was hard reading this because I had no idea the extent of their grief at the time:

"I'm empty, I don't like to talk about it anymore because the more I talk the less there is left inside of me. The more I fake it, the more numb I get to real emotions but not only am I meant to be the happy one, I am meant to be everyone's rock.

I supposedly have friends, hundreds of them but none of them know what I go through, none of them ask what I go through, and none of them have the time to check in and listen to what I am going through.

I am stuck in a world that I don't feel a part of, I feel the tunnel of darkness getting longer with little holes of light here and there but no way out.

I feel my family around me supporting me but in my head all I am to them is a burden, I am their biggest worry, I am why they don't sleep and why they come home exhausted and stressed. I love them and they know that but I'm numb and nothing fixes numb.

I listen to everyone saying "you're going to get through it" but the thing they don't understand is I'm sick of going through it.

Each hour that I spend without a distraction makes my mood fall darker and darker till I have reached the bottom of the pit, then the only way out is to cry enough to fill the hole back up and reach the top.

When you get to the top you try to drag yourself out, but, because the tears are only a temporary solution they dry back up and you keep falling back down into a cycle of pain."

There are no words to describe the pain you feel when someone you care about, someone absolutely incredible, is stuck in this spiral of grief. There is no way to pull them out of it, that is up to them. The only thing you can do is to care and to make it obvious that you care. Ask them how they're feeling, genuinely listen to them, and make sure they know you are there in any way they need you. It is not your job to fix their pain, because you can't. It is your job to help them see that life is worth living, the future is bright, and there is a way forward.

. . .

One of my closest friends, James, described grief as a full-body experience:

"It weighs on the chest, drains energy, and alters the rhythm of daily life. The brain struggles to reconcile absence, cycling through memories in search of something that no longer exists in the present. That's why grief feels so disorienting - it disrupts the way we once understood the world."

After reading this, I realised why I felt so disconnected from Bali after

Luna was gone, and even more so after I lost Olive. It's not that they just weren't there anymore. It's the hard truth that nothing felt the same, and could never feel the same there, again.

. . .

And Jackson shared something that really stuck with me:

> ***"Grieving isn't just about missing what was, it's about mourning what could have been. It's grieving the everyday things - the calls, the hugs, the simple routines you never thought twice about. The hardest part is realising you're moving forward without them."***

That's something I've struggled with too. With Luna and Olive, with the end of my relationships, with everything I've ever lost. The memories hurt, yes, but sometimes it's the future that hurts more - the version of a life you were supposed to have, the one you planned for, the one you assumed was yours.

. . .

But maybe the hardest truth of all came from the person who loved Luna and Olive as much as I did:

"Grief is the price we pay for love."

And that's it, isn't it?

Loss only hurts this much because we loved something deeply enough to allow it in. We don't grieve things we didn't care about. The deeper the love, the deeper the ache when it's gone. So maybe the goal isn't to avoid loss. Maybe the goal is to love in a way that makes all this pain worth it.

. . .

There was a time when I thought moving forward meant leaving the pain behind - like if I could just keep myself busy enough, distracted enough, I wouldn't have to feel it as deeply. But I've learned that grief doesn't work like that. You don't outrun it. You can't just ignore it until it stops existing. You can try, but it will always catch up with you, sometimes in the quietest moments when you least expect it. At first, I didn't know how to process losing Luna. I would wake up expecting to hear her paws on the timber sliding door of our villa bedroom, to feel the weight of her jumping up on the bed and resting on my leg. And when that didn't happen, there was this moment - just a second - where my brain would almost trick me into thinking everything was still normal, because I did enjoy life before Luna, right? But then reality would hit, and it was like losing her all over again.

That's the thing about loss - it doesn't happen just once. It happens in waves. First, the gut-punch of realisation. Then, the slow drip of memories, triggered by the smallest things - a familiar scent, an old photo, a place you once shared. You think you're fine, and then suddenly, you're not. What once felt so familiar, all of a sudden feels completely foreign and scary. For a while, I fought those moments. I told myself to be strong, to push through, to focus on the good memories instead of the pain. But grief doesn't work on logic. It doesn't care how much you know something is for the best, or that life has to move on. Grief demands to be felt. And eventually, I stopped resisting. I gave myself permission to grieve. To cry when I needed to cry. To feel the weight of it instead of pushing it away. And weirdly enough, that's when I started to move forward - not because the pain was gone, but because I stopped trying to fight it.

Researchers now reject the common idea of grief having "five neat stages." Studies from Columbia University show grief works more like a pendulum, swinging between moments of coping and moments of collapse. So if I laughed at a memory one day and broke down the next, it didn't mean I was back at square one, it just meant I was human.

I've been blessed with some incredible people in my life. The comfort I felt when I broke down in front of my mum, the ease I felt just knowing that someone else understood my pain, the reality check I needed from my dad when my world felt like it was falling apart, and even the resilience I hold onto from my sister, watching how strong she has been through some of toughest moments in her own life. The truth is - there is no right way to grieve. Some people need to talk about it. Some people need to be alone. Some people throw themselves into work, while others struggle to do anything at all. And none of it is wrong. For me, my family and writing this book have been a huge part of it. This chapter? It's part of my healing. It's me trying to make sense of something that will never fully make sense. It's me letting myself feel it instead of pretending I'm okay when I'm not. But more than anything, I've learned that moving forward doesn't mean letting go. It doesn't mean forgetting or replacing or "getting over it." Moving forward just means learning to carry loss differently.

At first, it's heavy - it takes up all the space, makes it hard to breathe, makes everything else feel insignificant. But over time, your world grows around it. You learn to hold it without it crushing you. You learn to live alongside it. Loss, as devastating as it is, changes us. It sharpens the way we see the world. It makes us softer in some ways, and harder in others. It forces us to appreciate the people and moments we still have. It teaches us to love deeper, knowing that nothing is guaranteed. I think that's why pain matters. Because it reminds us of what's real. It strips away the noise, the distractions, the things we thought were important but really don't matter at all. It forces us to ask ourselves: What do I *truly* care about? And maybe, just maybe, that's how we keep moving forward - not by leaving loss behind, but by letting it shape us into people who love harder, live fuller, and appreciate what we have while we have it.

. . .

Making Space for Loss

I don't have all the answers. I don't think anyone does. But I do know that loss isn't something you just move past. It stays with you. And maybe that's okay. Maybe we're supposed to carry the people and things we've loved, even after they're gone.

Grief is what takes the place of love when the anchor is no longer there. All of the love you still had to give now has nowhere to go, so it becomes grief instead. It's like the lost potential of what should have been but is no longer. And, it doesn't shrink, but your life does eventually grow around it. At first, I didn't understand what the concept meant. When you're in it - when loss is fresh and raw - it feels all-consuming. Like it's too big to ever fit inside the life you once had. But then, somehow, life stretches. It makes room. Not by erasing the grief, but by allowing and creating space for it alongside everything else. Alongside laughter. Alongside new love. Alongside moments of pure, unexpected joy. Because the truth is, grief and joy aren't opposites. They co-exist, tangled up in ways that don't always make sense. I've had some of my most gut-wrenching cries in the middle of a day that otherwise felt okay. And I've laughed, genuinely laughed, on days I thought would be unbearable. That's what loss does. It reminds you that life is both things at once. The love and the pain. The presence and the absence. The memories that hurt and heal all at the same time.

> Research shows that most people do eventually adapt. Not by forgetting, but by reorganising their lives around the loss. This is known as "integrated grief." The pain doesn't vanish, but it stops dominating every corner of your day. Life stretches to make space for it.

That's why I want to do something different to close this chapter out. On the next page, you'll find blank space. Maybe you'll write about someone or something you've lost. Maybe you'll write about the grief you're still learning to live with. Maybe you'll write one word, or maybe you won't write anything at all. Whatever you choose to do with it is up to you. If you do choose to write, I hope it gives you space to process. To acknowledge. To carry your grief in a way that doesn't weigh you down but reminds you of how much you've loved. Because if there's one thing I'm learning, it's that loss doesn't just mark an ending. It marks a new beginning as well. A beginning where you carry that pain differently. Where you let it shape what's next, but not define what is. Where you allow it to soften you instead of harden you. Where you keep moving, not because you've "moved on," but because love, real love, never leaves. It just changes form. And maybe, if we're lucky, we learn to carry it with a little more grace.

Not so quick...

If something stuck from this chapter, if a belief was challenged, or a certain thought made an impact - this is where you might want to take a second to reflect on it.

Write it down if you want to, or just sit with it for a few seconds.

Is What I Know Actually So? (Trauma Dump Edition)

Think of the last significant loss you experienced - a time of immense grief and uncertainty.

Now, ask yourself:

If grief never fully disappears, how can I carry it in a way that still allows me to love fully?

Then, *write about that experience.*

It doesn't have to make sense, but I do want you to sit in the place you've been avoiding...

Why?

Because that place is exactly where the real healing happens.

This space is for your thoughts.

Allow yourself to feel, allow yourself to hurt, allow yourself to write…

Chapter 6

THAT'S NOT LOVE

From the moment we hit our teenage years, we're bombarded with messages about what love and romance are supposed to look like. Movies show us grand romantic gestures. Social media feeds us curated versions of picture-perfect relationships. Porn serves up a fantasy version of sex that looks nothing like reality. And somewhere in the middle of all that, we're meant to figure out how to actually be in a relationship, how to explore our own desires, and how to navigate intimacy without completely losing ourselves in the process.

If you grew up in the age of social media, you probably know this pressure all too well - that pressure to be experienced, confident and in control when it comes to relationships and intimacy. But no one talks about how awkward it can be. How clumsy and confusing and human those first experiences often are. No one tells you that even the most confident people feel insecure in their own skin sometimes, or that relationships don't come with a manual, and that sex isn't a performance, even though everything around you makes it look like it should be perfect every time.

For me, this pressure showed up early. There was this unspoken timeline

I thought I had to follow - when I should have my first kiss, when I should have my first real relationship, when I should lose my virginity. And every time I fell behind that imaginary schedule, it felt like proof that something was wrong with me. I thought I had to be effortlessly confident with girls, to know exactly what to say and do, to have this whole suave, masculine energy that I'd only ever seen in movies. Meanwhile, in reality? I was overthinking every text message, worried about how I looked, and wondering if everyone else had read some secret relationship textbook that I'd missed.

And before we go any further, let me say this clearly:

If you're in that space right now - unsure, inexperienced, overthinking everything - you are not behind. You don't need to "catch up." You don't need to be more experienced to be worthy of love. You are already enough.

This feeling didn't disappear when I got into relationships either. If anything, it got louder. I wanted to be the perfect boyfriend - the one who always knew the right thing to say, who never got jealous or insecure, who was good in bed without ever needing to ask questions or admit I was nervous or simply couldn't 'get it up.' I put so much pressure on myself to perform that I completely missed the point of what intimacy was meant to be: messy, imperfect, vulnerable. And I know I'm not the only one. The more conversations I've had with mates and the more honest my DMs have gotten, the clearer it's become that so many of us feel like we're faking it. We're pretending to be more confident, more experienced, more secure than we actually are, because admitting we're still figuring it all out feels embarrassing.

But here's the thing: *everyone is still figuring it out.* There's no finish line after which you suddenly become the perfect partner or the ultimate lover. And the more we chase that illusion, the more disconnected we become - from ourselves, from our partners, from the kind of love that actually feels fulfilling. That's what this chapter is about: unpacking the pressure, getting honest about how it's shaped me, and finding a way back to something real.

. . .

Relationships. Oh yes, good fun aren't they? I've experienced a few since the ripe old age of 16, and it took some reflecting, but somewhere along the way, I realised something uncomfortable:

I wasn't just looking for love.

I was looking for validation.

Being chosen made me feel valuable. Being in a relationship made me feel complete. And when I wasn't, I felt like something was missing.

At first, this subconscious need for validation was reasonably harmless, but what started as curiosity quickly became a deep-seated anxiety about the future. I was influenced by pop culture at a young age into thinking that I should have the best-looking girlfriend because that was a sign of success. I was made to think it was cool to have a girlfriend so I'd always be talking to someone, we'd become 'boyfriend and girlfriend' for a few weeks, and then inevitably I'd get dumped or I'd get bored and either way I'd move on to the next. I wanted to experience it all because I thought that would also make me fit in with my friends - from my first kiss at 12 to losing my virginity at 16. But, on the flip side of that, I also had expectations that I wanted to uphold to respect myself and my innocence. I didn't just want to have sex with anyone, I wanted my first time to be with someone I cared about. I didn't want to be known as a fuckboy so I'd try not to talk to multiple girls at the same time. I'd always try my best to be a gentleman, no matter the circumstances. I'd make sure her feelings were heard and I'd always strive to be the best partner I could be. As a teenager, and even as a young adult, my true identity felt complete when I was in a relationship; and when I wasn't, I was trying as hard as I could to be 'marriage material.' I thought of myself as a better person when I was in a relationship and this is where I let my expectations take over...

For 4 years of my life, from the age of 17 to 21, I was really into this girl from my high school. The specific desire to have her in my daily life changed significantly over those 4 years, but no matter how it changed, I was always chasing something unattainable. I saw her for the first time at a high school party. She immediately stood out in a room full of friends and classmates, but none of us boys had the courage to speak to her. At the end of the night, I saw she was sitting with her friend waiting to go home. I went over and sat near them. I started talking to her friend and learned that they hadn't booked an Uber yet, so, being the gentleman I am, I offered to book them an Uber.

On the surface, this looks like a slightly strategic, but kind gesture from a teenager who genuinely cared about these two girls he barely knew. And despite recognising that I may get a few brownie points, in truth, it was an honest gesture. I was raised in this way. My parents, my grandparents, and my whole family have always taught me to be kind, respectful, generous, and selfless. If another human is in need, it is my duty to help them. Despite my efforts to make a good impression, she didn't really talk to me after that night. A few weeks later, I saw her at a party again. My best mate and I had been talking about her all week and in our infinite 17-year-old 'I-own-the-world' wisdom we made a bet - the first to kiss her wins. I don't even think there was any money on it, just ego and bragging rights.

Spoiler: it backfired horribly.

He won. He got the girl. But, my ego couldn't let that slide, so I decided to intervene. I interrupted their little party kiss and word got out pretty quickly that we had made a bet on that kiss. I felt awful. This girl was very sweet, had great morals, and was just trying to enjoy high school parties like the rest of us, and we'd disrespected that. We both apologised the next week at school. I was still very keen on this girl and I guess I saw winning her trust back as a bit of a challenge. That night kicked off a cycle I didn't recognise at the time - one where my worth became tied to whether or not she picked me. Long story short, she pursued my friend for about 6 months, they had a little party fling every weekend but nothing really eventuated. She actually went on a date with me during those 6 months, but I didn't get a second date.

This weird little love triangle came to a head on the day of my 18th birthday. My mate came over early to help me set up for what was sure to be one of the best parties of the year, and we spoke about her again. We came to an agreement that we wouldn't let her stand in the way of a great night and we both promised not to approach her out of respect for each other. Night time came around fast. The party was pumping, everyone was having a great time. We'd done the birthday cake and I'd skulled a few beers to keep the crowd happy. Then, I looked over to my right and I saw them on the couch together. And, in my young, drunken state I decided I wasn't happy with that so I let them know what I thought. Next thing I knew, she was telling me she just ended the weird little fling they had because she was interested in me now. This was the start of a 3-year relationship that taught me so much about myself, about love, about family, and about the way people grow and change in early adulthood. All of a sudden, I went from a stupid teenage boy to a young man who had to prove he was worthy of a strong, independent young lady. She was headstrong, knew where she wanted to go, had great values, and was truly committed to giving this relationship a go. And the first 12 months was an incredible journey of new experiences. But, there were a few key things I didn't think about at first, which ended up causing a turmoil of confusion for me.

. . .

One of the hardest things for a young person is to truly allow themselves to be open to their own intimate desires. We've spent our entire childhood thinking that sex and intimacy is something to be embarrassed about, and that's made even more prevalent if your parents 'forbid' anything remotely related to dating and relationships. In our late teens, the majority of us are having many 'firsts.' First real feelings, first sleepovers at a partner's house, first intimate moments, first fights, first big breakups, etc. When the rules our parents set for us as teenagers deprive us of those experiences, we feel the need to rebel against that, but it takes a mental toll. I did everything I could to create an environment where she felt safe and comfortable to explore those curiosities. But, knowing now what I didn't understand then, it didn't matter what I did - every moment she spent with me felt like a step towards rebellion against her parents, against those who cared about her the most, because having a boyfriend was made out to be a *bad* thing.

The truth is, she became my world, but I was never fully welcomed into hers. I started to feel like I wasn't a good person, or like I wasn't good *enough* for her. I began to feel dirty for wanting to explore intimacy with a consenting adult in a respectful and caring environment. I can't fully express how hard this was for me, everything felt incredibly confusing and I could never quite figure out why. And it all meshed together to create a 3-year chase for something that would never exist - approval.

How could I expect the girl I loved to approve of me, if her own father didn't?

And as a result, this constant yearning for approval changed me.

I went above and beyond to prove my worth.

I lowered my standards for what I was willing to accept in the relationship.

I became ashamed of my own intimate desires.

I lost my sense of self.

Funnily enough, science says this chameleon act is actually quite common. One set of experiments showed that people literally changed their self-image to mirror traits of someone they're into. They even started adopting the other person's not-so-great habits just to feel closer to them. And if your self-esteem's in the gutter, you're even more likely to absorb a partner's bad traits along with the good.

I even changed my physical appearance to fit her idea of the 'perfect' man - to the point where she would tell me that she likes the look of tattoos on a guy, so I'd start looking at tattoos to get.

And all of this turmoil had a profound effect on my mental state. Sex was taboo and a rarity, so when it did happen, I felt the need to make sure it was good. Again, I was desperate for approval. I needed our relationship to feel so right, it outweighed the guilt she felt being with me. And because of all this, I would experience so much anxiety around intimacy that I'd either last all of 5 seconds or I wouldn't 'get it up' at all…

And let me tell you, there is one sure way to completely mess with a 20-year-old's confidence:

Make them think their body is broken.

I wish I was joking. I fully believed that I was broken, and that rattled me. Every time it happened, I felt like I'd done something wrong. I didn't know how to fix it and I sure as hell didn't know who to speak to about it. I thought I couldn't tell my friends because they'd judge me, I thought I couldn't tell my parents because they wouldn't understand, and I thought I was the only one experiencing these issues so I guess that meant I was on my own.

> The truth is, surveys conducted by *Onebright* found that almost 60% of men actually avoid sex due to performance anxiety. In fact, experts stress that issues like this are extremely common - a lot more guys struggle with it than ever let on in public

I experienced this for months and it took a huge toll on my confidence, so eventually, I started doing some research about how to fix it. I read about premature ejaculation and erectile dysfunction being quite normal and common in young men (all men, in fact) and that started to make me feel a little better. I also read that most of the time, this was either caused by unhealthy lifestyle habits or a range of psychological factors. I was an active, fit and healthy young bloke so I knew it wasn't my lifestyle causing these issues, which meant it must be psychological.

I was one of the lucky ones growing up. I never thought talking to a psychologist was taboo. Truth be told though, the idea of talking to someone about my performance in bed was still terrifying. Eventually, I got to a point where I simply thought I couldn't solve it on my own. I wanted to talk to someone about it, but I found it:

- Quite challenging to organise an appointment with a good psychologist, and;
- Incredibly expensive for a 20-year-old who was studying full-time

So I just did what most blokes do. I tried to fix it myself… and I tried *everything.*

Numbing cream to last longer - which just made sex feel clinical. It killed the spontaneity and only made me more self-conscious.

Then I tried *"delay" condoms*. They sort of worked, but they also dulled the whole experience - physically and emotionally.

Eventually, I turned to the big guns: prescription pills from a men's health app. *Viagra* for the confidence, then *SSRIs* for the stamina (not at the same time). And yeah, they technically worked. But at what cost? I was timing pills before date night like it was a science experiment. I'd either be wide awake at 3am with a splitting headache and a hard-on that wouldn't quit, or I'd feel emotionally flatlined.

Sex turned into a chore - one I felt like I was failing at if I didn't plan it perfectly.

All of these 'bandaid' solutions kind of did what they were supposed to do, but they ruined the entire experience for me, and for her, and I could feel the relationship dying because of it. I did end up speaking to a psychologist about those issues in bed. He helped a lot. I also did end up speaking to my dad about it. He helped a lot too. He actually told me that he'd experienced similar issues throughout his 20s (sorry for outing you, dad). I spoke with my friends about it, they too had experienced the same thing. And one of my brothers. It seemed like the thing I was embarrassed about the most, was the thing most people around me were experiencing as well - and not one of us really wanted to admit it.

This whole 'perfect alpha male' narrative is exhausting - and fake as hell. In our 20s, these experiences are all new and exciting and scary and fun, and yet, we're made to believe that we should be perfect from day 1. It's backwards. And, you know what's funny? After that relationship ended, I went on a few first dates. Low in confidence and unsure if I'd last 5 seconds, 5 minutes, or even get it up at all… naturally, I didn't really want those dates to end in bed. But, inevitably, it happened. And the first time, it wasn't great. I had worked it up so much in my head that the act was basically finished before it even started. But, as they say, I was back on the horse…

It was this experience that made me realise I was free. No more expectations, no need to perform, nothing to live up to. If it was bad, oh well, move on. I could feel my confidence starting to come back, I was actually enjoying dating and I was finally having fun again. The anxiety didn't vanish, but it started losing its grip. It would still happen every now and again, but rather than seeing it as a failure, I started viewing it as just a thing that happened. I told myself it was fine and I'll try again in the future - no biggie. Realising I wasn't broken, just human, felt like finally taking a gasp of air after holding my breath for years. I felt like I'd finally got my power back and that did absolute bits for my self image. The teenager who didn't enjoy life without a girlfriend was now completely unbothered whether he was with someone or not. It was freeing.

And sure enough, that's when I met the girl who would be the most important part of my next chapter - right when I least expected it. When you find a love that is genuine, without expectation and without guilt, everything feels easy. You grow organically, you explore new things with joy and openness, you communicate, you work through problems together, you build a life that matters. And this time felt different in every way. Yes, I let anxiety creep in at times and yes, it has an effect, but it wasn't the overarching narrative of this relationship. For the first time, I felt like I was doing love the 'right' way. Like I had finally figured it out - and even still, that relationship wasn't meant to be… but I'll tell you more about that in a later chapter.

. . .

I've learned, against common belief, that true confidence comes from honesty. From knowing who you are without needing to perform. From being able to say, "Yeah, sometimes I get in my head," or "I don't really know what I'm doing either," and being okay with the reaction. The more I tried to be perfect, the more disconnected I felt - from myself, from my partner, from the actual experience of love and intimacy. I was ticking boxes, chasing validation, trying to live up to an image that didn't even belong to me. And for what?

To impress people who weren't even thinking about me?

To convince myself I was 'doing it right'?

That's the biggest trap, I think. Believing that perfection does exist. Like there's a perfect level of competency you're supposed to hit before you're allowed to feel worthy. But the truth is, relationships don't work like that. Sex doesn't work like that. People don't work like that. Real connection comes when the mask comes off. When you're not trying to impress, or prove anything, or hide the parts of yourself that feel a bit awkward or uncertain. It comes when you can say, "I'm a little nervous," or "Can we slow down?" or "I don't know if I'm ready for this," and to be met with compassion instead of shame. That's intimacy. That's safety. That's love. And I know how rare that feels when you're still looking for it. But you don't need to have it all figured out to deserve something real. You don't need to have a six-pack or a perfect track record or a wildly confident sex life. You just need to show up as you are. I promise, that's enough. Even if it doesn't feel like it. Because the right person will see it.

There's something incredibly freeing about reaching the point where you no longer need to perform. Where you don't have to impress the person in front of you or live up to someone else's expectations. Where you realise that being a good partner isn't about flawless execution - it's about presence. It's about effort. It's about the ability to be honest, even when it's messy. I still have insecurities. I still have moments of doubt. But now, instead of seeing those things as a sign of weakness, I see them as proof that I care. That I'm human. That I'm showing up in a way that's real. And maybe that's the underlying point of this chapter. Not to say "here's how you fix it" or "here's what to do next" - but to say:

You're not broken. You're not alone. You're not unworthy.

You're just human, trying to navigate the wild, confusing, beautiful mess that is relationships and intimacy and self-worth.

So, if no one's said this to you before, let me be the first:

You don't need to be perfect.

You don't need to have all the answers.

You don't need to perform or pretend.

You just need to be honest - with yourself and with the people you choose to share yourself with.

That's what real confidence looks like and that's what real intimacy feels like.

Not so quick...

If something stuck from this chapter, if a belief was challenged, or a certain thought made an impact - this is where you might want to take a second to reflect on it.

Write it down if you want to, or just sit with it for a few seconds.

Is What I Know Actually So?

Think about your idea of the 'perfect partner' or your idea of what a 'perfect love life' might look like.

Now, finish this sentence:

I feel like I am:

a. Already living up to these ideals.
b. Nowhere near these ideals.
c. Becoming these ideals.

Then, ask yourself:

Has chasing that perfection actually brought me closer to love, or has it built a wall between me and the potential for real connection?

Chapter 7

ADDICTED TO LIKES

We all know social media is bullshit… and yet we still fall for the trap. Every time we open an app, we're served an endless stream of people doing more than us.

More *fun.*

More *money.*

More *love.*

More *life.*

And no matter how grounded or self-aware we think we are, something about it still messes with our head. Not because we don't know it's curated, but because it's curated so well. You see someone's business hit 7-figures and start questioning why yours feels like it's crawling. You see your friends in long-term relationships and wonder why you can't even get past the talking stage. You see someone's body transformation, their "soft launch" of a new partner, their holiday cocktails or designer bags or podcast interviews or promotions at work, and somewhere in your brain, you start to question your own life. You start to believe the lie that you are falling behind. Social media doesn't show the in-between. It's not designed to. It rewards attention, not mediocrity. So, we don't see the panic attacks or the quiet doubts, the months of being broke or lonely or confused, unless it has a good hook... We only see the curated bits - the highlights, and sure, sometimes the lowlights, but regardless, you're only seeing what they're allowing you to see.

Then there's this other layer. It's not just the consumption of content that's damaging, it's the lies within our own content as well. The way we've been taught to package our own lives in little digestible squares. Even when things are falling apart behind the scenes, we still think we have to look like we're thriving. We get addicted to the perception of having it together, even if it's just a facade. I've done it too. Posted wins I didn't really feel. Smiled through things I didn't really enjoy. Hidden the struggle just so I wouldn't seem like I was slipping. And it's exhausting. There were times I'd scroll through my own profile and think:

This isn't even me anymore, it's just the version I thought people wanted to see.

But the thing is, I know I'm not alone here. Everyone I speak to - friends, clients, family - they're all feeling the same way. Everyone's tired. Everyone's comparing. Everyone's trying to live up to a standard that is simply unachievable. And no one wants to admit it, because we're all part of the problem. That's what this chapter is about. It's about the illusion we've all bought into, and the damage it's doing when we let it shape the way we see ourselves. I'm not here to tell you to delete your apps or go off-grid forever. I'm just here to pull back the curtain a little. To tell the truth about what it's like behind the social media success. And hopefully, to remind you that your messy, real, unfiltered life is more than enough - even if it never makes it to the feed.

. . .

In high school, I used to think it was uncool to follow more people than the number of people who followed me. For example, if I had 654 followers and I was following 655 people, that was absolutely not cool and I had to do something about it. As social media grew in popularity, I began to enjoy the thrill of new followers flowing in. If I met a new person, I only considered our friendship 'real' if they followed me back, and if they unfollowed me at some point in the future, well I guess our friendship was over...

Influencers didn't really exist when I was first starting to explore social media. My first 1,000 followers were pretty much just friends from school, a few family members, and a random mix of boys and girls who I met at high school parties and either thought they were 'cool' or thought they were 'hot' - and if they were 'cool' or 'hot,' I'd usually follow them back. This was fun in high school. It gave my ego an artificial boost every time someone new followed me, and I guess I was lucky because I mingled with the 'popular' group which gave me many opportunities to meet new people and collect new followers. It was like a game. I became addicted. As I grew older, influencers started becoming a thing. I still remember the first time I saw someone I knew with over 10K followers - she was the older sister of a close friend of mine and I thought she was basically celebrity status with that many followers. When she followed me back, it felt extra special as if she was better than the other people who followed me simply because society voted that she was worthy of more attention.

I was brainwashed to believe in this notion that *social media followers = real-life value.*

And I started seeing people differently depending on how many followers they had.

Influencers continued growing in popularity and before I knew it, I was spending hours on Instagram every day just scrolling through posts from accounts with hundreds of thousands of followers who were seemingly living a lifestyle that most people only dream of. This consumed me. If I was stuck at school every day, I guess I found an escape in living vicariously through these influencers. My follower count sort of stagnated around 2,000-3,000 people during high school, but the number of people I followed continued to grow and grow. My only criteria for following someone?

"I want what they have."
→ *clicks follow*

And seeing all of this idealised content made my life feel better for a while. But, eventually I felt envy start to creep in. I was no longer grateful for the life I had and noticed myself wishing it away. I was so incredibly lucky to have the upbringing I did and I'm still blessed to have such an amazing family supporting everything I do - and yet, social media still to this day makes me feel like my life is not good enough, like I am not good enough.

There was a very clear point in my adolescence where I realised how impactful social media truly was, and how fine the line between good and bad actually is. It started with my finance obsession at 16. I would spend hours at the computer and on my phone trying to learn as much as I could. Because of my newfound interest, I noticed my Instagram feed started becoming increasingly more educational. This felt weird. I guess I was so used to a feed of pure entertainment that I didn't even know I could use social media to actually learn useful information and build positive habits. This was the switch that helped me escape the matrix - even if just for a moment. As I got older and started realising that I could curate my own social media feed to deliver real value, not just to make me feel like my amazing life wasn't as amazing as the next guy's amazing life, I began to understand the importance of intention on these platforms.

Practically everyone on social media is a consumer - whether we admit it or not, even those who create content, consume just as much, if not more. In the creator world, we often call it 'research' when scrolling on TikTok for hours as if we're looking for the next viral video idea that will make our account blow up - but really, we're just consuming like everyone else. These apps have won the attention game. They suck us in and there's nothing we can do to stop it. But, we can do a good job of helping ourselves by choosing ahead of time what we want to see. And look, I get it, you don't want to unfollow someone because it might offend them and well 'what if I see them again some day?'

Truth is, my Instagram now follows maybe 5% of the people who follow me and a handful of influencers/brands who genuinely add value to my life. I did what's called a 'cull' or a 'cleanse' and I felt damn good doing it. It can be hard to unfollow people who you feel emotionally obligated to remain in contact with - but realistically, if you saw them in public, would you even say hello? These are the questions I now ask myself when deciding who to follow and who not to follow:

1. If I saw this person in public, would I say hello?
2. Does this person's feed make me feel happy, jealous, envious, wiser or bored?
3. Do they post interesting content, often?
4. Does this person seem authentic, or not?

Oh, and if they're so close to my inner circle that they definitely would get offended if I didn't follow them back, then sure I might give them a few extra points. But ultimately, there are plenty of people who I do not follow who I know are probably offended that I do not follow them. And similarly, there are plenty of people who I follow who don't follow me back and if I really thought about it, I probably would get upset by that. But the fact of the matter is - this is my life and I will control the elements I have control over. I can't control the actions of other people, but I can control what I see online and I will do all I can to make my social media addiction a positive one, because let's be real - we're *all* addicted.

. . .

The mindgames we play with each other on social media are embarrassing to admit out loud, but you're lying if you say you haven't played them. I remember being fifteen, heartbroken for the first time, and thinking the smartest thing I could do was post a mysterious photo of my friend's pink nails to make it look like I was hanging out with a 'new girl.' Not because I was necessarily attracted to her, but because I wanted my now-ex to see it and think:

Wow, he's moved on already!?

Meanwhile, I'd sit there refreshing the story views, heart racing, hoping, praying that she'd see it and feel sorry enough to message me. Of course she didn't. And even if she had, what would that have changed? Nothing. I still would've gone to bed that night feeling empty. And I guess this is something we learn as we grow older, we think if I can just look happy enough, seem fine enough, pretend I've got my shit together enough, it'll manifest into the truth. Unfortunately, that's not how life works. You need to fight every day for mental peace, and sometimes the necessary work is hard and exhausting and downright scary, but this is the price of true happiness.

The next few years of my life basically turned into a series of performances. Subtle ones. Not over-the-top. I wasn't staging fake photoshoots in a private jet or pretending to live some wild life I wasn't actually living. I was doing something much more common, like:

Posting a quote about growth after a breakup to seem like I was handling it well.

Sharing a picture of the latest self-help book I was reading to look deep and unbothered when really I couldn't focus on a single page.

Tagging my location at a party I didn't even want to be at because the right people might see it and think I was out there living.

It's wild how much effort we put into convincing people who aren't even thinking about us that we're doing just fine. And honestly? It worked. People thought I was confident. Independent. Thriving. Meanwhile, I was overthinking everything, wondering if I was falling behind some invisible life timeline, hating myself for caring so much about likes and views and who watched my stories first. I used to wait hours to reply to people, too. Even when I was desperate to talk to them. Because somewhere along the way, I learned that showing you cared too much made you look needy. So instead of sending a reply whenever I saw the first text like a normal human, I'd stare at my phone like an idiot, setting alarms in my head: wait twenty minutes. Now an hour. Make it seem like you're busy. All just to create the illusion that I was someone worth chasing.

The funny part is, now I am busy. Some weeks I genuinely forget to reply to people for hours, sometimes days, because I'm too caught up in living the life I used to pretend I had. I'm not saying this to sound smug.

I'm saying it because the whole game is rigged from the start. When you're young, you think you're supposed to look impressive. When you mature a little, you realise you're supposed to be impressive, but mostly just to yourself, not to people you barely even know. There's this part of me that still clings onto the performance sometimes. I won't lie about that. There are videos that I've deleted because they didn't sound "hooky" enough. There are posts I've pulled down because they didn't get enough likes. Even though I'd love to sit here and pretend that stuff doesn't affect me anymore. It does. But, not in the same way it used to. While it may affect me, it doesn't control me anymore. It doesn't dictate whether I feel proud of myself anymore. But it does still poke at the little insecure part of me that wants to be seen, wants to be validated, wants to feel like what I'm doing matters. And maybe that's just human. Maybe we're not supposed to be completely immune to that. The difference now is that I don't let it shape what I create.

I don't post just to prove something.

I don't delete things because they didn't perform the way I'd hoped.

I don't measure my worth in shares or saves or stupid little love hearts on a post.

I don't waste time trying to craft a life that looks good online if it doesn't feel good offline.

...

When I started building Uncle Nathan, everything changed. Suddenly, social media wasn't just about flexing or being seen. It was about building something real. Something valuable. At least, that's what I told myself. But even then, the lines got blurry. There were times when everything was flowing - videos going viral, news articles being written, podcast downloads spiking, follower counts growing by the thousands. And then there were times when it felt like I was shouting into the void, pouring my heart out and getting nothing but crickets in return. That contrast was exhausting at first. Because somewhere deep down, I still derived my value from my followers, from how large the digital applause was. It wasn't enough to know I was building something important. I needed other people to see it, too. Otherwise, what was the point? Now let me tell you, that's a dark road to walk down. Especially when you're spending eight, nine, sometimes ten hours a day on social media trying to build something bigger than yourself, and you feel like you're getting nowhere.

It's weird how easily you can start to measure your entire life in numbers and notifications. But the truth is, no amount of growth is ever enough if your self-worth is still tied to external validation. I had to learn, often painfully, that my value doesn't increase just because my follower count does. And it doesn't decrease when my engagement tanks. The work matters because it's my work. The life matters because it's my life. Not because anyone clapped for it, but because I said I wanted to do something, and I did it. Still though, I won't pretend I'm above it. Even now, when a post goes viral, it feels good. Of course it does. I'm not a robot. It's satisfying to see something you made resonate with people. It's validating to feel seen. And it's normal to enjoy that. The problem is when your whole sense of self depends on it.

I've been there. I've felt that dopamine crash when a post doesn't perform. I've doubted myself after one slow week. I've questioned whether I should change my style, my voice, my whole online identity just to fit whatever the algorithm seems to want. It's exhausting. It's never-ending. And it's a trap. You can't build a real life chasing fake applause, and you can't create real impact by measuring your worth in views. Some days, the thing you post that feels "small" will matter more to someone than the viral hit you spent three hours planning, 2 hours shooting and 5 hours editing. You just won't always see it right away. That's the real difference between building a life for the feed and building a life for yourself. One is an endless treadmill. The other is a long, winding, beautiful road. And yeah, it's slower. It's messier. It's quieter. But honestly, at least it's real.

. . .

Another thing no one tells you: A small circle is a good circle. There's this idea social media quietly feeds us - that the more people you know, the more worth you have. That your value is somehow tied to the number of names in your DMs, the number of replies to your story, the number of group chats you're in, or how many comments you get when you post something vulnerable. But here's what I've come to believe: that is not connection. It is just noise. I used to think being liked by everyone was the goal. That the broader my network, the more followers I had, the more 'worthy' I'd feel. And sometimes, yeah, it did feel good. But it fades. And what's left behind is this weird *hollowness*. Because surface-level attention isn't the same as actually being seen. A hundred people can reply to your post, and you can still feel completely alone.

I noticed it when I was living overseas. Bali is a beautiful place and can present some incredible opportunities, but it is also a very transient experience. Every connection you make is temporary, every person is on their own journey and you might be part of that for a few months but eventually they'll go somewhere else and you'll be left alone again. It's hard to build a core group of friends in a place where everyone is coming and going, a place where everything feels fleeting. And I did make some great friends in Bali. But very few I would consider inviting to my wedding, or expecting to show up at my funeral. What I've come to realise, especially in the moments where life gets heavy, is that you don't need a crowd. You need a few people who actually know you, and love you. People who text you when you go quiet. People who've seen you at your lowest and still show up. People who care about who you are when you're not performing.

Social media makes it easy to mistake *proximity* for *closeness*. Just because someone watches your story doesn't mean they know anything about you. Just because someone replies "proud of you" doesn't mean they'll be there when shit hits the fan. We forget this sometimes. A small circle is not a bad thing. It keeps you grounded. It keeps you accountable. And more importantly, it gives you room to grow without having to perform. When you've only got a few people in your life who truly matter to you, you stop wasting energy trying to impress people who were never going to care in the first place.

Evidence actually suggests there's an optimal small group size for emotional support. One research summary reports that about 3–5 close friendships is ideal - enough to prevent loneliness and depression - and that "more is not always better." In fact, people with very large social networks (say 15 or more close friends) often feel more lonely, because spreading their attention so thin reduces how deep the connection can be.

Don't get me wrong - I still love meeting new people, still believe in building community, still share things publicly. But the older I get, the more I realise that not everyone should get a front-row seat to my life. Not everyone deserves that kind of access. The more noise you strip away, the more you can actually hear yourself think. And in a world where everyone's shouting to be seen, that silence is powerful.

. . .

I've tried to write this chapter from the middle of it. Not from the mountaintop looking down, but from the messy middle where I still check the likes, still feel the sting of a post flopping, still get caught up in someone else's aesthetic life and wonder if mine stacks up. This isn't a chapter written with distance and perspective. It's written in real time, while I'm still figuring it out. And maybe that's the point. I'm trying really hard to keep this book from becoming a self-proclaimed, guru-speak excuse for giving unwarranted advice. But if you take anything from this chapter, please take this:

Social media is not real life.

You know that, and I know that.

But it's not enough to know it.

We have to act on that knowledge.

That means we have to actually stop comparing our raw, unfiltered life to someone else's curated highlight reel.

Stop measuring our self-worth in views, likes, shares, saves.

Stop building our life to be seen by others instead of loved by you.

Start chasing alignment instead of followers.

Start asking what matters to you, not what will impress other people.

Start building a life that feels good on the inside, even if it looks boring on the outside.

Not everything has to be content. Not every moment needs a caption. Not every win needs a post. And no, your iPhone camera does not need to eat first.

You don't need to be "seen" to be real.

You don't need to be "liked" to be worthy.

You don't need proof that you exist.

You just need to live.

Wholly and without applause. Because I've learned - slowly, painfully, and honestly - that life doesn't happen in the post-worthy moments. It happens in the moments you don't think to share. The moments that are too quiet, too sacred, too imperfect for the feed. Where no one's watching, but you're still showing up, still growing, still becoming. And those are the moments that matter.

So if this chapter has done anything at all, I hope it's helped you come back to that. To remember that your life is allowed to be unpolished. It's allowed to be peaceful and beautiful and unseen. It's allowed to be yours. Live more of that life. Even if no one ever double-taps it. Actually, especially then.

Not so quick...

If something stuck from this chapter, if a belief was challenged, or a certain thought made an impact - this is where you might want to take a second to reflect on it.

Write it down if you want to, or just sit with it for a few seconds.

Is What I Know Actually So?

Think about the last time you scrolled through Instagram or TikTok and heard that inner voice whisper "I wish that was me."

Now, finish this sentence:

I often notice an overwhelming sense of ____________ when I see posts from _________.

Then, ask yourself:

Has following that person/account ever actually made my life better - or has it only pulled me further into comparison?

Chapter 8

BREAKING DOWN QUIETLY

Before we get into it, I want to make something clear. This chapter is going to focus heavily on men's mental health. That's not because I think our struggles matter more or women don't face equally devastating battles. It's because I'm a man, I'm not a subject-matter expert, and I can only speak from my own experience. So this isn't about figuring out who has it harder. This is about acknowledging that there is a specific kind of silence around male pain that desperately needs to be broken. And if you're a woman reading this? Please don't skip it. This chapter might be written through a male lens, but it's just as much for you. Whether you're a sister, a girlfriend, a daughter, a wife, or a friend - the men in your life are probably struggling with things they feel they can't say out loud. My hope is that by being brutally honest in this chapter, I can give you a deeper understanding of what that silence looks like on the inside, and why it's so important that we start talking about it. Because the reality is, men are dying in that silence.

We don't talk about it enough. Not in our friendship groups. Not in the media. Not in the football dressing rooms or at work or in our own homes. Men are taught to toughen up, to "man up," to keep it together. We're praised for our stoicism, rewarded for our emotional control, but when that bottle eventually bursts, the fallout is devastating. I understand that this subject is incredibly sensitive and I want to make sure I approach it with the level of care and perspective it requires. The thing is, what I've experienced and felt is going to be completely different to what you've experienced and felt. But, regardless of how unique each of our experiences are, there is one undeniable truth:

This is an epidemic.

It is quite literally tearing families apart, and I can't shake this feeling of helplessness in and amongst it all. This chapter is not going to be a five-step guide to fixing your mental health. I don't have that. But, what I do have is the opportunity to speak directly to you. To tell you that what you feel is valid, that your fear is warranted, and that, together, we can affect real, positive change in this world.

. . .

I grew up in a house where love wasn't something you had to earn. It was just there. Constant. Unconditional. I never got told to "man up" or "stop crying." If I was upset, I was allowed to be. No one tried to make me feel stupid or sweep it under the rug. And that's rare. Especially for boys. My dad was my role model. He was tough in the football dressing room but at home he was gentle. He wasn't afraid to show emotion. I saw both versions of him, and I'm so grateful for that because I also saw what the outside world expected from him. Football demanded a different kind of man. Composed. Stoic. Switched on despite what may have been going on behind the scenes. I noticed early on that being soft didn't always have a place. There were spaces where vulnerability was welcomed, and then there were the rest, where it wasn't. Then my parents split and everything shifted.

I was nine years old and suddenly I wasn't just a kid anymore. I was "the man of the house." At least that's what it felt like. No one said those words to me directly, but they didn't have to. When your world splits in half, you start looking around for the glue. You start asking yourself: *if not me, then who?*

Mum did everything she could to protect my sister and I from the pain of it all. And she did a very good job, too. But there were moments. Moments that stay with you. Moments where I didn't know what to do, where I just stood there, frozen. And even though I was nine, even though I couldn't possibly understand the weight of everything she was carrying, I still felt like I should've done something. Like I should've been able to fix her pain. But I couldn't. And that made me feel weak. Dad was coaching the Central Coast Mariners and had moved up to Terrigal for work, which was about an hour and fifteen minutes drive from mum's house. We only saw him every second weekend. I know he struggled with the distance, I could feel it, but I don't remember seeing him cry. I guess it was the moments we weren't there that were the hardest for dad. And I wanted to fix that for him, too. Maybe I could go live with him? But then I'd be leaving Mum, and I couldn't do that either. It felt like no matter what I did, someone I loved would be hurting.

I was seeing a school counsellor during that time. I honestly don't remember much about those sessions, but I do remember the feeling of them. I'd walk in feeling confused, heavy, numb. I'd cry a lot. But, I'd walk out feeling like maybe it was okay not to have the answers yet, that maybe I didn't need to carry everything with me all the time. Looking back, those sessions were probably the first time I learned that emotions aren't something you "deal with" but rather, something you move through. A year or so later, both my parents found their forever partners. My stepdad, Pete, came into my life and flipped everything I thought I knew about "manly men" on its head. Ex-military. Rough around the edges. Handyman-kind-of-guy. But also the softest, most emotionally aware man I've ever known. He hugged me like he meant it. He gave advice when I didn't ask for it but needed it anyway. He told me when I fucked up, and he told me when I made him proud. He never got mad at me, because that was still my dad's job, but he was never afraid to show up fully for my mum when he needed to.

To have two father figures who were so different in style, but the same in love - that's something I'll never take for granted. A lot of boys never get one. I got two, and I count myself lucky for that every single day. My step-dad taught me that vulnerability and responsibility aren't opposites. That you can cry and still be strong. That you can be scared and still act in alignment with your values. But he also taught me that being a man isn't just about feeling, it's about stepping up when it matters. It's about doing the hard thing. Making the call when no one else wants to. Being the one who carries the weight, not because you have to, but because you can. And that stuck with me.

I don't think we talk about this enough. Resilience is a *muscle*. You've got to train it. It doesn't get stronger in comfort. It grows through reps. Life throws you curveballs and every time you get back up, you teach it to continue those behaviours. But even the strongest lifter needs a spotter. Tell me one person who's hit a new PB in the gym without a spotter or support crew...

That's right - it's unheard of.

So, if resilience is a muscle, why do we try to go through life without that spotter?

The truth is, every time life levels you up, it also throws a harder challenge at you. The struggle doesn't get easier, you just get stronger. Or at least, you try to. It's like a fire-fight that never ends. You put out one blaze, and another one starts. And some days, you're so burnt out from the last battle that even lighting a match feels dangerous. Unfortunately, this is life. You don't win by staying upright the whole time. You win by getting back up again. And again. And again. But let me say this clearly - asking for help when you're trying to get back up again doesn't make you weak. It makes you human.

In my experience, one thing I have noticed more times than not is that our world continues to mistakenly reward the illusion. If you look like you're doing well, if you seem functional, people don't ask questions. You can be an absolute mess on the inside and still get praised for your "resilience." You can be quietly falling apart, unable to leave the house, and everyone thinks you're just "busy" because you're not reaching out. That's the trap. We're taught that if we're productive, we must be okay. If I'm still showing up to work, still going to the gym, still making conversation, then I'm all good. No one checks in on the guy who looks like he's coping. And for a long time, I bought into that. I thought if I could just keep performing, if I could keep moving fast enough, I'd outrun the ache. But you can't outpace your own mind. You can't hide from it forever. The hard bit is, it doesn't always show up as sadness or tears. Sometimes it's numbness. Sometimes it's anger. Sometimes it's apathy (that feeling where you're not even sure what the point of anything is anymore). I've had days like that. Days where everything feels heavy for no reason. Days where people tell me how "well" I'm doing and I nod, smile, thank them, and yet, feel completely disconnected from the version of me they think they're seeing. That disconnect can eat you alive.

So if you've felt it, I just want you to know that you're not the only one. You're not weak for feeling it. And the mask? You can take it off. You're allowed to be real.

. . .

Something that has been a quiet companion in my life for about as long as I can remember is anxiety. I know it's a word we throw around a lot, almost like it's trendy, but it's something I think we need to discuss. For me, social settings were the worst. I'd get invited to a party and my stomach would drop. Not because I didn't want to go, I did. I just couldn't stop the whisper in my mind telling me I'd say the wrong thing, or look stupid, or get laughed at, or not know where to stand or who to talk to or how to act. Sometimes I pushed through. A lot of times I let those negative thoughts win. And while I've gotten better at dealing with it, even now, in my twenties, I can feel that same churn in my gut when I walk into a room full of strangers or even a room full of friends. That urge to run still shows up. The difference is, now I've got the tools to deal with it. And those tools? I didn't figure them out on my own.

I've always been a huge advocate for therapy, for speaking to someone who's trained to walk you through the chaos in your head. Not just venting, but unpacking. Digging deeper than just "I'm feeling anxious" and figuring out where that's actually coming from. Look, I know therapy isn't perfect. It's expensive. It's hard to access. It's stigmatised as hell - especially for men. I'm far from a credible source on this, but in my opinion, I think we've got it backwards in this country. You can walk into a GP and get antibiotics for a cough in 10 minutes, but if your brain's unwell? Good luck waiting six months for a bulk-billed appointment with someone who may or may not even understand you. And don't get me started on how therapy is still seen as some last resort for people who are completely falling apart. Like you have to be on the brink of total meltdown to deserve help, as if needing support means you've failed at coping. Quite frankly, it doesn't make sense. We need to normalise therapy for the every day struggles too - social anxiety, breakups, performance pressure, not knowing what to do with your life. Not just full-blown episodes. Because the truth is, most people who end up in crisis didn't get there overnight. It was drip-fed. A slow unravel. And maybe, if someone had helped them sooner, they wouldn't have reached that point at all. I get it - we also have a supply issue in Australia. There simply aren't enough therapists. I can appreciate that it's a complex challenge with many variables and stakeholders. I wish it was an easy fix, but I understand that it's not. That's why I've got so much respect for grassroots mental health movements like Gotcha For Life, Tomorrow Man, The Good Human Factory, and even the more informal stuff like run clubs, walk groups and surf meetups. I find it's those smaller initiatives that are really driving change. It's not about fixing everything. It's about giving blokes a space to just chat shit with other blokes, without needing to be "on" all the time. Even that alone can be life-saving.

Recently, a friend of mine's boyfriend launched a boys' walk club in Sydney. Every Sunday morning, a bunch of guys show up, walk, and talk. Deep or surface-level, it doesn't matter. It's a circuit breaker. And I reckon we need a thousand more of those popping up around the country - because psychologists are booked out, blokes are bottling it up, and we're losing too many of them to silence. It doesn't take a degree to help someone feel heard. Sometimes all it takes is asking, "You having a good day today?" and actually listening to the answer. Not the autopilot "Yeah, you?" version. The real answer. And if they brush it off, you ask again. You check back in. You notice the changes. You don't wait until it's too late. Unfortunately, sometimes we can do everything right and it's still not enough. But, simply being the kind of person someone feels safe enough to talk to in the first place can be the difference. Because feeling heard feels good, and it can quite literally turn an "I can't do this" into a "Maybe I'll give it one more shot." You've got fathers, brothers, partners, friends. You've got men in your life who will never open up unless someone makes it okay to do so. And you can be part of that shift. You can be the one who notices. The one who listens. The one who makes it safe. We all play a role here. Because mental health isn't just a binary scale between "fine" or "fucked." It's a spectrum. Some days are lighter. Some days are heavier. But none of it is static. None of it is linear. And no one is immune.

Someone I've met through my podcast journey who does incredible work in this space with The Good Human Factory, Cooper Chapman does a great job explaining how we should view our mental health:

> Cooper says "Your mental health is like a bucket. Every time you deal with something hard - stress, conflict, grief, disappointment - it pokes a new hole in that bucket. Slowly, your energy leaks out through those holes. And unless you patch them up with something strong, no matter how hard you try to refill the bucket, eventually, you will tire and your bucket will drain completely."

The scary part is that most guys will keep trying to pour into other people's buckets even when theirs is bone dry. Because we're taught to provide. To protect. To show up no matter what. But what good are you to anyone else if your own tank is empty? You cannot pour from an empty bucket. So, you've got to patch it up first, and then you've got to fill it back up. Sometimes, you have to protect your bucket like your life depends on it (because it literally does). And if you're not sure where to start? Start small. Ask the question. Reach out to a mate. Join that walk club. Book the appointment, even if it feels scary. Even if you don't know what to say when you get there. Because silence won't heal you. But connection might.

. . .

I know this chapter may have felt heavy. I didn't write it to sound inspirational. I wrote it to be honest. Because the truth is, men are struggling - and most of them are sitting in silence. We carry the weight and say we're fine. We break and call it "just a rough patch." We ache then laugh it off. And we do it because somewhere along the line, we were taught that's what strength looks like. To bottle it up. To harden up. To keep going, even when we're barely holding on. But real strength isn't silence. Real strength is owning your mess. It's crying when you need to. It's admitting, "I'm not doing great right now." It's picking up the phone and saying, "Can you talk?"

If you're a guy reading this, I want you to hear me:

You are allowed to struggle.

You are allowed to feel lost.

You are allowed to lean on support.

And you are no less of a man for saying so. In fact, you might be more of one for having the courage to speak up.

And if you're not a guy - if you're someone who loves one - your role is just as important. Don't underestimate how powerful it can be to simply ask, to check in, to listen without trying to fix. Make it normal to talk. Make it safe to be real. And don't stop reminding the men in your life that they matter and their struggles matter too. This stuff can't be left to crisis hotlines and awareness weeks. It has to be woven into how we show up for each other every single day. Because the truth is, we won't fix this by telling men to "man up." We'll fix it by giving them permission to be human. And yeah, maybe this chapter leaned a bit more advice-heavy. Maybe I got a little blunt in parts. But that's only because I've seen what the fallout looks like when this conversation doesn't happen. And I've felt the shift that occurs when it finally does. So if you've been holding something in, take this as your permission to let it out. You don't have to carry it alone. None of us should have to. And if you don't know where to begin, just start with a conversation. That's how change happens. Every single time.

Not so quick...

If something stuck from this chapter, if a belief was challenged, or a certain thought made an impact - this is where you might want to take a second to reflect on it.

Write it down if you want to, or just sit with it for a few seconds.

This is a permission slip, use it.

Complete this sentence, written or in your head:

One thing I've been struggling with recently is ______________________.

That's it. That's the start...

You don't need to do anything with it yet. Just let it exist outside your head for a minute.

Now, it's your turn.

Think about that friend who's always doing 'fine' so you never really feel the need to check in on them.

Write down one person's name here: ______________________________

Then, ask yourself:

When was the last time I checked in - like, really checked in, with them?

If it's been a while, send the message. It doesn't need to be deep - all you have to do is show up and listen.

Part 3

FIGURING IT OUT ANYWAY

Chapter 9

NO ONE CARES

We spend so much of our lives worrying about what people think of us. What they'll say. What they'll notice. How they'll react. We obsess over the smallest details - the shirt we chose, the post we made, the thing we said in that one conversation, replaying it all like people are dissecting our every move. The funny thing is, they're not. See, most people are too caught up in their *own* mess to care about yours. And the sooner you accept that, the sooner you free yourself. We like to believe we're on stage 24/7. Like our life is some kind of performance and the audience is watching, waiting to judge and ridicule you. But the truth is, most people aren't thinking about you at all. Not because they don't like you. Not because you don't matter. But because they're too busy thinking about themselves, just like you are. Let that sink in.

The pressure you feel to succeed, to look good, to post the right thing, to be the person you think everyone expects you to be - that pressure isn't real. It's self-inflicted. It's a mental prison built out of assumptions. You think everyone's watching, but no one even remembers what you posted yesterday. I mean think about it… try to specifically recall 2 standout Instagram stories you remember seeing yesterday. My bet is you can't. So why are you wasting your life trying to impress people who aren't even looking? This chapter is about realising no one actually gives a sh*t and how that's the best news you'll ever hear. Because if no one's really watching, then you don't have to perform. You don't have to be perfect. You don't have to look like you've got it all together. You don't have to curate your life for the imaginary audience in your head. You just have to live. You just have to do what feels right. And once you stop living to impress people who aren't even paying attention, you'll finally have space to figure out what you actually want, not what looks good, not what sounds impressive, not what gets the most likes. Just what's real. Because that's where life gets good again.

. . .

It's wild how many things I've done, or not done, purely based on the assumption that someone might be watching. Not *is* watching. Might be. Maybe. Possibly. That's all it takes. This little made-up voice in my head starts running commentary on everything I do. What I wear, what I post, how I walk into a room, who I date, what I say at the end of a conversation - all of it gets filtered through this lens of "what will people think?" It's exhausting. And the worst part is, it's mostly in my head.

I remember being 11 years old and getting selected for the gifted and talented program at school. It was a big deal, especially because I was one of the only Year 5 kids chosen when it was usually reserved for Year 6s. I should've been proud. And I was. But with that came this sudden weight, like now I had to prove I belonged there. Like I had to keep being the smart kid because people were now watching. I was no longer just a kid in the classroom. I was the one expected to be ahead. And I carried that for years. Every report card. Every test. Every award. I chased them not just for the accomplishment, but for the feeling of being seen as "still worthy." Still living up to the idea people had of me. I was terrified that if I slipped up, even once, it'd all unravel. And it didn't stop at school.

I moved to a new high school in Year 11 and didn't get an invite to our academic awards night that first year. After being DUX two years in a row before that, it felt like a punch in the gut. I felt embarrassed, even though no one said a word. Even though no one would have noticed. But in my mind, they were all watching. So in Year 12, I went harder than ever. I wanted to win everything I could - and I did. Best all-rounder, sports awards, academic awards, the works. Don't get me wrong, I was proud of those wins. I worked for them. But if I'm honest, they weren't just for me. They were to prove to everyone else that I hadn't failed to reach my potential. That I was still the person they thought I was. That I was worth noticing. It's easy to look back on that now and see how much of it was built on assumptions. The truth is, most people who attended that awards ceremony were there for themselves or their own son/daughter. They wouldn't have even noticed my awards. But at the time, it felt like everything mattered. Every single detail. That's the thing about the spotlight effect, it's not that people are watching. It's that we convince ourselves they are, and then live as if it's true.

There's this Jay Shetty quote I heard once that hit me hard:

I'm not who I think I am.
I am who I think you think I am.

It sounds like a riddle, but it's exactly how we live. We walk around shaping our identity based on the version of ourselves we assume other people are perceiving. And the wildest part? We're probably wrong about that version most of the time. We're building an entire self-image around someone else's imaginary opinion.

It turns out that most people greatly overestimate how much others notice them - a bias psychologists call the spotlight effect. In classic experiments, people wearing embarrassing tee shirts vastly over-predicted how many observers would remember the shirt's image. In truth, audiences focus far less on us than we imagine. Research explains this by showing we tend to "anchor on our own rich experience" and adjust insufficiently for others' perspective, which means the mental spotlight is usually far dimmer than we fear.

Social media makes this even worse. I used to overthink every post. Like, painfully overthink. I'd write a caption and then rewrite it six times.

I'd pick a photo and then scroll back to compare it with my "aesthetic." I've literally changed outfits five times before leaving for a party just in case someone said something, only to arrive and realise no one was even paying attention to which version of a black t-shirt I wore. We want to be seen so badly, but we're terrified of being seen the wrong way. It's a weird contradiction - craving validation but also fearing judgement. And in the middle of that contradiction, you lose track of what you actually want. You post what's expected. You dress for the aesthetic. You shrink when you want to speak, and perform when you want to be real. It's not always conscious. Sometimes it's just a subtle filtering of yourself. A soft censorship you're not even aware of. There have been countless times I've stopped myself from promoting things I'm passionate about - my business, this book, the stuff I've worked hard on - purely because I didn't want to come across as 'that guy.' I didn't want people to think I was full of myself, or trying too hard, or simply doing a bad job. So I said nothing. Held back. Even though I believed in it. Even though it mattered to me.

That's how powerful perception can be. The fear of what people might think can silence the things that mean the most to us. And yet, in most cases, those people aren't even thinking about you at all. Or if they are, they're probably comparing themselves to you, wishing they could be more like you. The truth is, they're worrying about their own outfit. Their own post. Their own awkward text reply. They're thinking about what you think of them. It's this hilarious loop of imagined judgement where no one's actually judging, everyone's just terrified of being judged. And it took me a long time to understand this. I had to take the risk that people were watching, in order to learn that they weren't. And in that space between comfort and ridicule, I realised that I'd made the whole thing up. It's not as if this realisation instantly frees you. But it does start to unravel the lie. It makes you question where your choices are coming from. Are you doing this because you want to? Or because you think someone expects you to? Are you avoiding this because it doesn't feel right? Or because you're scared of how it might look?

This is the tension I still sit with. I don't have it figured out. I still catch myself wondering how well something might be received. I still hesitate before sharing parts of myself and I still think twice before saying what I really want to say. But I'm getting better at noticing it. And sometimes that's enough. Because once you stop trying to impress an audience that isn't really paying attention, something beautiful starts to happen: You get to do things for you. Not for applause. Not for clout. Not for the made-up scoreboard in your head. Simply because they matter to you. And that's when your life actually starts to feel like yours again.

. . .

It's strange how many people assume I have my life together. I get it - I've lived overseas, I've built businesses, I've traveled, I've been in relationships, I post content that's polished enough to look "intentional." From the outside, it probably does look like I figured everything out early. Like I'm doing something right. But that's the thing about perception: it's curated without effort. People connect dots that were never meant to be connected. What they don't see is the behind-the-scenes. They don't see me second-guessing every major life decision I make. They don't see the quiet panic I feel when my business slows down. They don't see the fear I had about moving back to Australia and wondering if that'll look like I "failed" the Bali dream. They don't see the nights I spent crying after my breakup. They don't see the days I feel like a fraud or the weeks I don't post, not because I'm too busy, but because I'm too anxious to put anything online. Perception is shiny. But, reality is just... well, human. And that's probably true for a lot of people we admire. We assume those who look successful must feel successful. But you can have all the pieces - the money, the freedom, the lifestyle - and still sit at home wondering if you're doing any of it right. It's like walking around in this costume that says, "I've got this," while your inner voice is whispering, "You're winging it and eventually someone's going to find out."

This persistent self-doubt is called *impostor syndrome*. Research describes it as a pervasive sense of intellectual or professional fraudulence among high-achievers. In other words, despite real accomplishments, people with impostor feelings can't internalise success and fear being exposed. Studies confirm many talented individuals attribute their wins to luck and live with anxiety that one day they'll be judged unqualified.

Imposter syndrome isn't just for new grads or people starting fresh. It follows you. The more you grow, the more you feel it. You think, surely someone more qualified should be doing this. Surely I'm not the best person to speak in this meeting, to run this workshop, to offer this advice. Every time I step onto a stage to talk about life or mindset or self-worth, a part of me wonders if I even believe what I'm saying. Not because I don't mean every word - I do, but because there are many days I won't even take my own advice. I would spend hours crying on the floor of my Bali villa wondering if I'd built the wrong life for myself. I would look at my girlfriend, our puppy at my feet, the rice field view from the balcony, and think: *Why do I still feel empty today?*

It wasn't every day. But it lingered. And it's scary when everything looks right, but something still feels off, because then you start to question yourself. Am I ungrateful? Am I broken? Is this just who I am now? But the truth is, none of that makes you broken. It just makes you human. And what's even crazier - no one knows you're thinking these things at all. To everyone else, you're doing great. People message me for advice like I've figured out some secret sauce in life. They see the podcast clips. The speeches. The lifestyle. They don't see me changing outfits six times before going to a dinner because I'm spiralling about something dumb like whether my shirt makes me look strong or skinny. They don't see me hovering over the "post" button on an Instagram reel for 20 minutes wondering if I'm about to be judged or ignored. And look, maybe this sounds dramatic. But it's real. This is what it means to live under the illusion of perception. You become aware of the gap between how people see you and how you see yourself, and the bigger that gap gets, the more disoriented you feel.

It's lonely, honestly. Because when people think you're thriving, they stop asking if you're okay. You don't fit their mental image of someone who struggles. And so you play along. You nod. Smile. Say things are "great." Sometimes, it's easier to perform than to try and explain the mess in your head - especially when you don't fully understand the mess yourself. And in all of this, you still think people are watching. You still think they'll notice if you slip. You still think they'll whisper if you scale back the business, or pivot directions, or move home, or post less. You think they'll clock your "failure" like it's headline news. But the truth? Most people won't even think twice about your next move. Not because they don't care, but because they're living in their own filtered reality, just like you. They're trying to keep their own life together. They're worried about what you think of them. They're overthinking their own relationship, their own career, their own timeline.

> And cognitive psychology actually supports this: we naturally centre on our own perspective and often fail to fully account for what others see. Classic attention studies show that when people focus on one task, they can miss obvious things happening right in front of them. In everyday terms, this means if I trip over my words, most listeners will probably be preoccupied with their own thoughts, not examining every detail of what I'm doing or saying.

I recently learned of an amazing example of this. It's called 'The Invisible Gorilla' experiment. In one of psychology's most famous experiments, researchers asked people to watch a short video of players passing a basketball and count how many passes were made. Partway through, a person in a full gorilla suit walks through the scene, beats their chest, and walks off… and 50% of the viewers completely miss it (yes, that's HALF). They don't even notice a gorilla on the screen! It's wild.

The experiment shows how our brains filter information based on what we think is important. We focus so much on our own task or our own anxiety, our own self-image, that we miss the obvious: everyone else is doing the same. So, when I say, no one notices - I mean it. Your massive wins. Your public humiliations. No one is paying as much attention as you think. Even the big things fade. Let's ponder - how many people in your life have had a failed relationship? A stalled business idea? A breakdown moment? You probably remember the general vibe of it, but not the specifics. You might've thought about it for a day or two, and then life moved on. That's what people do. We just move on. So when you obsess over how something might look, just know this: the spotlight is mostly in your head. You are not the complete centre of anyone's universe. And that's not a bad thing. That's freedom. Because if no one remembers your failures as deeply as you do, then maybe it's safe to try. Maybe it's okay to risk looking stupid and to post something you actually care about, to change direction publicly, or to let go of the act.

Maybe "having it all together" isn't the flex we thought it was. Because now, more than ever, people are tired of perfect. They're tired of polished. They crave real, messy. Proof that it's okay to not have all the answers. And you can only give people that proof if you're brave enough to live it. Not in an inspirational "look at me being vulnerable" way. But in a quiet, steady, unapologetic way. In a way that says, "Yeah, I'm still figuring it out too. And that's fine." Because even when it looks like you've figured it out, you still wake up wondering if you're doing any of this right. And I think more people need to hear that. Not to feel better about themselves. Not to put you on some self-aware pedestal. But just to feel seen and understood in the most basic of ways.

. . .

I'm not writing this because I've cracked the code. I still slip up. I still fall into old patterns, overthink what I post, question my choices, wonder if people are judging me, or if I'm screwing everything up without realising it. I still get caught in that loop. But this part of life, the realisation that no one's actually watching as closely as you think, it's the one thing that's consistently brought me peace. And of everything I've learned so far, it's the lesson that has truly stuck with me. So, I'm not sharing this to preach. I'm sharing it because it helped me. It changed how I show up. And if you're anything like me, if you've spent a bit too much of your life performing for people who weren't even paying attention, maybe it'll help you too. Because here's the real takeaway. You spend years, maybe decades, shaping yourself for an audience that doesn't even exist. You micromanage your personality. You post the curated version. You bottle up the weird shit you love and put on a front that feels safer. And for what? For people who forget your Instagram story the second they scroll past it? We all do it. It's human. But once you understand that no one's really watching, everything gets lighter. You stop playing to the crowd. You stop hoping for applause. You stop performing a life that isn't even yours. And what you're left with is… you. Messy, unfiltered, figuring-it-out-as-you-go you. The person who doesn't have all the answers, who sometimes backpedals, who still gets anxious at parties and worries about being misunderstood, but shows up anyway. That's someone worth being. And someone worth being around.

So this isn't advice. This is just my reminder - to myself, and to you too - that you don't have to get it right. You just have to live in a way that feels like yours. Because the people who matter? They don't need the polished version. And the ones you thought did? They were never really paying attention to begin with. You don't need to impress people who aren't even looking. You just need to be someone *you* can live with at the end of the day. And maybe that's the whole point. Because no one actually gives a *shit*. And thank *fuck* for that.

Not so quick...

If something stuck from this chapter, if a belief was challenged, or a certain thought made an impact - this is where you might want to take a second to reflect on it.

Write it down if you want to, or just sit with it for a few seconds.

Is What I Know Actually So?

I want you to think of one embarrassing moment you've had in the last year.

This moment was embarrassing because ______________________________.

Then, I want you to think about one embarrassing moment a random friend has had in the last year.

Can't remember any?

So, why do you think anyone else remembers yours?

Chapter 10

BLOW IT ALL UP

Today, I walked away from a relationship I thought would last forever…

There's a quiet ache that follows a decision like this one. It doesn't shout. It doesn't come rushing in like a wave of panic. Well, maybe sometimes, but generally, it just… lingers. It shows up in the quiet moments. In the stillness after the chaos. When the tears have dried, the bags are packed, and the space you once shared is empty again. That's where I'm writing from right now. This passage isn't going to be clean. It's not going to wrap up with some neat lesson about how everything works out in the end. Because honestly, I don't know that for sure yet. I'm still in the middle of it. Still figuring it all out. What I do know is this:

Sometimes the most loving thing you can do is leave.
Even when it breaks your own heart.

Breaking up with someone you love is not the same as falling out of love. I think that's what people forget. Love can still be there, pulsing under every word, every hug, every shared memory, and you can still know, deep in your bones, that it's time to go. I didn't leave because I stopped caring. I left because I could no longer recognise myself. And until I loved myself again, I could not love anyone else. I know how dramatic that sounds, but when you're in a relationship, especially one that feels all-encompassing, your sense of self becomes entangled in it. And over time, without even realising, you start making decisions not based on who you are or what you want, but on who you think you should be to keep the relationship working. That's not her fault. It's not anyone's fault. It's just what happens when you love someone deeply... you bend. You shift. You compromise. But eventually, I bent so far I couldn't remember what my own life looked like anymore. The clarity I used to have, about my goals, my future, my identity, it all became foggy. And I kept telling myself, "It's just a phase. I'll get it back. It's just burnout, or stress, or growing pains."

But it wasn't. It was a slow realisation that the path I was on wasn't mine anymore. I started to feel like I was watching my life happen instead of living it. Like I was playing a version of myself who looked happy and successful and in love, but underneath it all was this gnawing sense of confusion. Not only about her, but about me. About who I'd become and where I was going, and whether I could really offer someone else a happy life when I didn't even know what kind of life I wanted anymore. So I did the thing I was most afraid of doing. I left. Not because anything was majorly wrong. But because I needed to feel right again.

22.06.2025

...

The truth is, we all come to forks in the road. Moments where life hands us a decision we didn't feel ready for. A moment where we realise something has to change. But change isn't glamorous. It's not the "new year, new me" energy you see on TikTok. It's sitting on your bathroom floor at 1am with no idea how to explain to the people around you that the life you've built isn't working anymore, and you don't even know why. Sometimes, it's walking away from something good - a job, a friendship, a relationship - simply because you are no longer the person you were when you chose it. Other times, it's choosing to stay when everything in you wants to run, because deep down, you know there's something here worth fighting for. And either way, it's hard. We've been taught to equate clarity with confidence. To only take big risks when we're 100% certain. But life rarely gives you that luxury. Growth doesn't wait for clarity. It demands courage. It asks you to move even when your legs are shaking. And that's the uncomfortable part about making a self-honouring decision: You don't always get to know if it was the right one. Not right away. Maybe not ever. Sometimes, all you get is a quiet knowing in your chest that says, "This matters to me. Even if no one else understands it."

And that's where most people get stuck, not in the knowing, but in the fear that follows it. The fear of disappointing people, of being misunderstood, of giving up something that still has some good in it, and the fear of what comes next. We don't talk about this enough:

> You can be grateful for something, and still know it's not aligned anymore.
>
> You can love someone and still know you're not ready to show up for them fully.
>
> You can have a job that pays the bills, and still know you're destined for more.

We tell ourselves that making hard decisions needs some dramatic justification, like something has to be really wrong for us to walk away. But sometimes the only thing that's 'wrong' is that you've outgrown the person you used to be. And to call that 'wrong' doesn't make sense at all. But, it's enough of a reason to leave. It's enough of a reason to pivot. And it is more than enough of a reason to start again if you want to.

Usually, the hardest part isn't the decision itself, it's the emotional aftermath. The loneliness that comes with going against the grain. The silence after you've finally spoken the truth. The mental weight of second-guessing everything, even after you've committed. But here's something I've come to believe wholeheartedly:

There are only two paths in life.
There is simply: living your truth, or avoiding it.

And living your truth doesn't always make you feel better straight away. Sometimes it makes you feel worse because it's asking you to let go of comfort and certainty, to let go of the known version of your life. But it's also asking you to trust yourself. To believe that who you are becoming matters more than what you're walking away from. It's hard to explain that kind of trust to someone who's never had to rebuild from scratch. But if you're reading this and you've felt it - that ache of leaving something that once felt like everything - then I want you to know this:

You're not broken for struggling with it.

And you're not crazy for choosing it anyway.

In fact, some of the strongest, most grounded people I know are the ones who've made the hard call without knowing where it would lead. My parents ended their marriage after 13 years and 2 kids, and they both subsequently found the love of their life. My childhood best-friend quit his trade after 4 years of apprenticeship to chase a lifelong acting dream overseas. My sister cut ties with friends she loved but no longer aligned with the person she had become. And these people around me didn't just do it because they were brave. They did it because not doing it hurt more. And that's the threshold most of us face, when the discomfort of staying becomes louder than the fear of leaving. When the voice inside you that says "I can't keep living like this" finally drowns out the one that says "But what if it's a mistake?"

That tipping point? That's where change begins. It's not loud or cinematic. It's not even visible to most people. But it's the beginning of a new chapter, even if you don't know the title yet. I say this all the time, but it's worth repeating:

We desperately try to find the breakthrough,
without experiencing the breakdown.

But the breakdown is often the doorway. And if you're someone who's standing at that door, scared, unsure, grieving and confused, I want to offer you this:

You don't need to have the whole staircase figured out, you just need to see the first step and take it. You don't actually need permission or proof that it will work. And, you don't need everyone to understand you, either. You just need to choose you. Choose the version of yourself you want to become. And when it feels too heavy to carry alone, come back to this. You're not alone. So many of us are navigating hard decisions right now - in private, in silence, in pain. But we're doing it because deep down, we believe there's something better waiting on the other side. Not better because it's easier. Better because it's *ours*. Our path. Our truth. Our life. And that, in the end, is what makes it all worth it if you have the courage to try.

. . .

I've had many moments where I've caught myself trying to rewind the clock. Wondering if I could've done something differently. If I should've stayed. If I gave up too early. But really, when I'm truly honest with myself, those questions aren't about regret, they're about grief. Grieving not just a person, but a version of myself that felt happy when I was with them. A version of me that had someone to share the weight of the world with. And now that I'm back to carrying it alone, I realise just how much I leaned on that connection - not out of weakness, but out of love, out of safety, out of the simple comfort of not having to figure everything out on my own. But maybe that's the point. Maybe there comes a time where you have to be on your own not because you want to be, but because you need to hear your own voice again. Because the noise of what's easy, or familiar, or expected starts to drown out the quiet knowing of your own gut. And eventually, you have to choose: keep going the way things are… or stop, risk everything, and rebuild. And honestly? I still don't know what the "right" answer is. I don't think I ever will. I just know that something inside me didn't feel at peace anymore. And I didn't want to wait until that internal tension turned into resentment, or until I started blaming someone else for a life I didn't have the courage to change.

Psychological research on decision-making actually shows that under pressure or ambiguity, people draw on emotion and intuition. In one study, time-pressure (which forces a more intuitive response) led individuals who were strongly fused to their partners to choose extreme self-sacrificing outcomes in a moral dilemma.

The older I get, the more I realise that courage isn't always loud. Sometimes it looks like disappointing people you care about, because you've finally stopped abandoning yourself. Sometimes it looks like crying in the car outside a house you no longer live in, knowing that walking away will hurt like hell… but staying would hurt quietly, for longer. And yeah, maybe it's selfish. But maybe it's also survival. I've been thinking a lot lately about how often we talk ourselves out of discomfort by convincing ourselves we can handle it. That we can adapt. That we can make it work. And sure we can, we're good at that. Humans, generally, are good at that. But what if that's not the point? What if the goal isn't to merely cope, but to thrive? In my experience, I've found that we typically choose familiar pain over unfamiliar hope. What I mean by that is, we'd rather continue living a life that feels misaligned, but familiar, instead of starting over in unfamiliar territory - even though in that uncertainty exists the potential for something greater than before. With that understanding, came the realisation that I don't want to get good at settling. I don't want to be the person who gets so good at making something tolerable that I forget I'm allowed to want more.

And I bet you've felt that too. Not just in relationships, but in jobs, in friendships, in cities you've outgrown but don't know how to leave. That whisper of "this can't be it," followed by all the fear of what it might mean if you listened to it. I think the problem is we expect clarity to arrive before we act. We want some thunderbolt of knowing to give us permission. But, what I've noticed throughout my life so far is that clarity rarely shows up first. Most of the time, it follows the decision - not the other way around. You don't know if it was the right call until months later, when your chest doesn't feel tight all the time. When your days start to feel spacious again.

When you catch yourself laughing in a way that sounds like you. And even then, it's not black and white. You can miss someone deeply and still know you had to leave. You can mourn a life that was good and still feel proud for choosing something uncertain. That's the complexity no one talks about - that sometimes the most self-honouring decision you can make will also be the most painful. I don't have steps for this. No dot-points. No five-part formula. All I can tell you is what I was telling myself every day for months: you don't have to have all the answers before you make the move. Sometimes the decision comes first, and the answers catch up. Sometimes you leap before you're ready because the longer you wait, the larger that distance between who you are and who you want to become grows. And maybe that's the most important thing I've learned through all of this, that self-abandonment doesn't always look dramatic. Sometimes it looks like nodding along when you want to scream. Sometimes it looks like planning a life that doesn't actually excite you anymore. Sometimes it looks like being so focused on not hurting someone else that you don't even notice the slow ache inside your own chest.

So no, I didn't feel certain. I didn't feel like a hero. I felt raw. And shaky. And a little bit numb. But underneath all of that, was something else too… a quiet kind of alignment I hadn't felt in a while. Like my inner world and outer world were finally starting to match up again, even if it hurt like hell to get there. I wonder if that's what it means to grow up? Learning to make the decision that's best for your future self, even when your current self wants to crawl back into comfort. Learning to sit with the silence that comes after honesty, and trust that it's leading somewhere better. Learning to choose the path that's yours, not just the one that feels familiar. And I guess another important learning in all of this is that pain isn't always a sign you've done something wrong. Sometimes, it's a sign you're finally doing what's right.

. . .

I don't know where this decision will lead me. I wish I did. I wish I could wrap it all up in a neat little lesson and say "it all worked out for the best" but I'm still in it. Still waking up some mornings wondering if I made the right call, if I'll ever find love again. But I think that's okay. I think we need to get more comfortable with being in the middle of things… in the murky, unresolvable parts of life where there isn't a clear hero or villain, where the ending hasn't arrived yet, and all you've got is your gut and the hope that it's leading you somewhere honest. What I've realised is that so many people are walking around with this exact same weight. Not necessarily about relationships, but about choices. The real kind. The grown-up kind. The kind that force you to stretch, and sacrifice, and step into uncertainty without any guarantees. No one really teaches us how to do that. We're taught how to achieve. How to plan. How to hold on. But no one tells us how to walk away from something good when it no longer feels aligned. They forgot to tell us that *grief* and *growth* often come holding hands.

In fact, breakup studies found that many people emerge stronger and more self-reliant after a breakup. One report found that the intense distress of a breakup can actually catalyse growth: anxious individuals who process their emotions deeply often report greater personal growth afterward. So really, while heartbreak disrupts our identity, working through the pain can actually rebuild a clearer sense of self and new purpose.

So if you're standing at your own fork in the road, stuck between what's familiar and what's calling you, I hope this chapter helps you to feel a little less alone. I hope it gives you permission to choose yourself, even when it hurts. Especially when it hurts. Because the truth is, the right decision won't always feel good straight away. Sometimes it feels like heartbreak. Sometimes it feels like failure. But deep down, you'll know when something's no longer right for you. And that knowing, no matter how quiet, deserves your trust. Maybe the point isn't to get it perfect. Maybe the point is to honour the version of you that's trying to surface, even if it means letting go of a version you once loved. If you're in that place now, questioning, aching, doubting, just know this:

You're not lost. You're becoming.

And sometimes, becoming requires breaking things that once felt unbreakable. You're allowed to choose the harder path if it's the one that sets you free. And one day, maybe not tomorrow or next month, but eventually, you'll look back and realise that this pain was the beginning of something true. Something that's finally *yours*.

Not so quick...

If something stuck from this chapter, if a belief was challenged, or a certain thought made an impact - this is where you might want to take a second to reflect on it.

Write it down if you want to, or just sit with it for a few seconds.

Is What I Know Actually So?

Think about that decision you've been avoiding: the job, the relationship, the city, the friendship...

Now, finish this sentence:

The reason I haven't made this change is because ________________________.

Then, ask yourself:

Is that a valid reason? Or is it just the excuse I tell myself to avoid the short-term pain?

Chapter 11

PERFECT IS POISON

There's something ironic in writing a chapter about perfection and rewriting the intro more than 3 times. I keep stopping and starting, shifting commas, second-guessing paragraphs, deleting full chunks of text and wondering if I'm saying too much or not enough. All while telling myself it has to land exactly as I want it to. That it needs to feel effortless. That people are going to read this and it has to be... I don't know... profound? But the truth is, I'll probably never feel like it's finished. And I guess that's kind of the point. This entire book has been a lesson in letting go. Letting go of perfection. Letting go of the book I thought it had to be. Letting go of the idea that something needs to be polished to be powerful. Because if I waited until it was perfect, until I felt completely ready, this book wouldn't exist. And that's not some inspirational quote I'm trying to turn into a mantra. That's just the truth. I nearly didn't finish this.

In fact, I nearly didn't start. I sat on the idea for months. Wrote 2 chapters in a day and then didn't touch it for weeks. Avoided it on days when I felt like I wasn't "wise enough" or "qualified enough" or "experienced enough" to say anything that mattered. But it kept pulling me back. Because I knew, deep down, there were things I wanted to say, even if I didn't say them perfectly. Even if I stumbled through the wording. Even if I changed my mind later. I don't know when we learn it, maybe it's school, or social media, or just this weird pressure that builds in the background of growing up, but somewhere along the way, we start believing that if it's not perfect, it's not worth sharing. That unless it lands with a bang, makes a splash, or breaks some imaginary standard of excellence, it's better left behind the scenes. And that belief will keep you stuck. It'll convince you to overthink things that never needed to be perfect in the first place. It'll whisper in your ear every time you try to do something bold: "What if it's not good enough?" And if you listen too closely, you'll talk yourself out of starting at all. I've lived inside that loop for most of my life. Still do, sometimes. I've always been a perfectionist. Not in the "I colour-code my closet" way (although I actually do that), but in the "I will spend six hours editing a 20-second clip and still feel anxious when I post it" kind of way. I care. Probably too much, and I've come to realise that caring too much can sometimes be the thing that stops you from doing anything at all.

That's what this chapter is about. Not perfection. Not success. Not even productivity. Just progress. Just the small, quiet, messy movement forward. Because honestly? Most of the big moments in my life started from places of complete uncertainty. I didn't have a plan. I didn't have a five-step strategy. I didn't even know what I was aiming for. I just had this gut feeling that something was worth pursuing, and I chose to move, even when it didn't feel like the timing was right or the idea was fully formed. Uncle Nathan was like that. My agency was like that. This book? Absolutely like that. You look back at these things and they seem like linear achievements. But the reality was Google Docs full of half-formed sentences. Nervous pitches where I made up answers on the spot. Videos that barely cracked a hundred views. And late nights wondering what the hell I was doing with my life. But I kept going. Not because I had it figured out. But because there was something in me that said, "just try." So no, this isn't a guide. I don't want to give you steps or slogans. I just want to tell you what I've learned by doing the thing before I was ready. I want to walk you through the mess, not just the highlight reel. Because progress doesn't always look pretty. And it never, ever feels perfect. But it's what gets you places. And sometimes, in fact most of the time, it ends up looking like the very thing you didn't know you were capable of creating.

. . .

I've always been a bit of a perfectionist, probably more than I'd like to admit. Not the textbook kind that's obsessed with symmetry or formatting, but the kind that overthinks everything, down to the smallest of details. If I'm working on something creative, I want it to look good. Not just good, I want it to look perfect. If I'm writing something personal, it has to say exactly what I mean, even if I don't know what that is until I've rewritten it six times. I don't like sharing things until they feel finished. But the problem is... nothing ever really feels finished. This book is proof of that. It's taken me almost two years to get to this point. More than 700 days of rewriting sentences, reshuffling chapters, cutting stuff that felt too safe, and forcing myself to lean into the parts that felt scary to write. There were many times I wanted to pause and come back when I felt more ready. Moments where I convinced myself it wasn't quite ready yet. But eventually, I had to accept that it probably never will be. Not because it's bad. But because I'm still learning. Still growing. Still figuring things out. And if I wait until I have all the answers, I'll never hit publish on anything.

> Studies into procrastination actually found that waiting to feel ready is usually why you feel stuck; action creates motivation, not the other way around. Experience and experts agree: you almost never feel 100% prepared, so progress comes from doing, not from waiting. In practice, simply starting the thing or posting the video, even if it's messy, often kick-starts learning and momentum, whereas waiting for perfect confidence usually means nothing ever gets done.

And that lesson hasn't just shown up while writing this book, either. It's a theme that has been made very clear in pretty much everything I've done. Especially everything I've done with Uncle Nathan. When I first started the Uncle Nathan project, I didn't really know what I was doing. I had this idea in my head for a platform that could help young people feel a bit less alone, a bit more seen, and a bit more hopeful about their future. But the reality? I wasn't some wildly successful mentor or guru. I didn't have all the answers. I barely had a following. I just had this gut feeling that I needed to make something that could help people. So I started. It was September 2020 when I first began working on it behind the scenes. I didn't tell anyone for months. I quietly built the website, wrote out some blog posts, and filmed a few videos in my bedroom. I didn't even publish anything until January 1st, 2021, because I was terrified it wasn't ready. Terrified that people would think, "Who the hell is this guy giving life advice?" And fair enough. I didn't really have the resumé for it. I wasn't rich. I wasn't famous. I hadn't travelled the world or started some million-dollar company. But I knew things. Things I wished someone had told me when I was 16. Things I'd learned through failing. And so I decided to share them, not from a place of authority, but from a place of honesty.

Learn with me, not from me.

That was always my mantra. And it still is. The early days were rough. In my first two months on TikTok I got maybe 100 followers total. I remember refreshing the app constantly, wondering if maybe I was just bad at this. Wondering if anyone would ever care. Wondering if I should just stick to my day job and leave it alone. But I kept going. Imperfectly. Clumsily. Publicly. And eventually, some momentum started to build. That little platform grew into something I never expected. Not just in numbers, but in impact. I started getting messages from people saying my videos helped them get through breakups. That my money tips helped them save for a holiday or a car. That my stories made them feel less alone. And slowly, I stopped obsessing over perfection and started focusing on building that momentum. The same thing happened with my agency. I started learning Meta Ads while working at a startup. I didn't study marketing at uni. I just learned by doing. Testing campaigns. Running low-budget ads. Figuring out what worked and what didn't. After a year, I quit and started my own agency. I had no idea what I was doing in the beginning. No real roadmap. No fancy client pitch deck. I just found people who needed help with their ads, charged what felt fair, and delivered results the best I could. It wasn't smooth. I fumbled through proposals. Undercharged for way too long. Spent hours watching YouTube videos just to answer client questions confidently. But I figured it out. One project at a time. One conversation at a time. And before I knew it, I'd built something that not only paid the bills, but gave me the freedom to move overseas and keep building.

Sometimes the only thing that separates people who "make it" and people who don't… is that the ones who made it just didn't stop. I don't think we talk about that enough. There's this myth that people who are doing well always knew what they were doing. That they had a 10-year plan and a vision board and a perfect strategy mapped out from day one. But most of the time, that's far from the truth. Most people are winging it and simply figuring it out as they go. The only difference? They keep moving. That's what I did with the podcast too. In the early days, no one was listening. I'd spend eight hours editing an episode and only my parents would tune in. It was hard not to feel like it was a waste of time. But I kept going. I knew the content was good, and I figured eventually, if people found it, they'd have something to binge. And when one of my TikTok videos finally blew up, that's exactly what happened. People didn't just listen to the one episode. They listened to all of them. They became actual fans. The compound effect is real, but it only works if you give it something to compound.

And honestly, that might be the most underrated part of progress: *consistency*. It's not the flashy stuff. It's the stuff that feels boring and repetitive. The stuff that doesn't go viral. The stuff that makes you feel like you're wasting your time. But behind every big moment, every "breakthrough," there's a million small moments that no one saw. That's how momentum builds. Slowly. Quietly. Then all at once.

> Psychologists actually talk about "small wins" as a key contributor to success: every little task you complete releases a burst of dopamine and kick-starts momentum. Basically, showing up regularly - even if your work is rough - compounds into real progress. Repetition and consistency literally make new habits more automatic, so imperfect effort every day is far more powerful than waiting to get it all perfect before you begin.

My speaking gigs were the same. The first time I got invited to speak, I nearly said no. I'd never done paid public speaking before. The thought of standing in front of 20 strangers, pretending to be qualified, made me sick with anxiety. But I said yes. Wrote the whole talk from scratch. Read it in front of the mirror a hundred times. Delivered it with my heart in my throat. And it landed. People came up to me after asking if I'd do another session. I couldn't believe it. Within a year, I was speaking in front of a room of 5,000 people. I felt like an imposter the whole time, but somehow, it worked. And that moment, that feeling of doing something I didn't feel ready for and nailing it anyway, stuck with me. It reminded me that no one really feels "ready." You just have to start.

There's a weird thing that happens when you begin to embrace imperfect progress. You stop waiting. You stop putting your dreams on hold until you feel more "qualified." You stop wasting time polishing things that should've been out in the world months ago. And you start trusting that you'll figure it out as you go. Because you will. Even now, I still don't feel like I have it all together. I have days where I question everything - my direction, my decisions, my ability to help anyone at all. But I keep moving. I keep learning. I keep shipping things, even when they're not perfect. Because finished is better than perfect. And imperfect progress is still progress.

. . .

Looking back now, it's obvious that everything I've built came from a mix of instinct, naive optimism, and blind momentum. Not strategy. Not planning. Not being "ready." Just showing up and doing the thing. What I wish someone helped me realise is that being unqualified was actually my superpower. There's a sense of humility in saying "I'm figuring it out too" that people trust more than someone pretending to have all the answers. And don't get me wrong, I had countless moments of wanting to give up. My first few TikToks flopped. I remember sitting there thinking, "Why the hell am I even doing this?" I felt like I was shouting into the void. But something told me to keep going. And I'm glad I did. Because all those early videos, the ones that barely cracked a few hundred views, built the muscle. They shaped my voice. They laid the groundwork for everything that came next.

People see the results now. They see the viral videos and assume it was an overnight thing. But I promise you, it wasn't. It was years of showing up, tweaking, refining, and not letting moments of success get to my head. If I'd waited until everything was perfect, Uncle Nathan wouldn't exist. This book wouldn't exist. And I'll be honest, I still don't always know what I'm doing. I just know that I've figured things out enough times that I can now trust myself to figure it out once again. That's the biggest difference between people who grow and people who stall. It's not their intelligence. It's not their network. It's not how "ready" they are. It's whether or not they're willing to be messy in public. Whether they're willing to be seen trying before they're good.

The Qatar World Cup was another perfect example of this. I didn't pitch myself as a content creator or build some master strategy. I just started filming vlogs because I wanted to show my sister what she was missing. That was it. No grand plan. Just a bit of footage and a vague idea that maybe people might like it. The first few videos blew up. Millions of views. Comments, shares, media coverage. Suddenly I was in the thick of something huge. I got opportunities, partnerships, gigs I never expected. But none of that would've happened if I hadn't filmed the trip just for the hell of it. It's insane to think how one tiny choice, to document something for my sister, changed the entire trajectory of my career. But that's the thing about imperfect action: you never know which move will be the one that shifts everything.

I've come to realise that perfection is just procrastination in a fancy outfit. It's a way to delay the uncomfortable part - putting yourself out there. Because if it's not perfect, you can still tweak it. Still hide behind the 'work-in-progress' sign. But sometimes, the thing you're trying to polish to perfection? It was ready 3 drafts ago. So, if you're holding back because you don't feel ready - good. That means you care. But do the thing anyway. Launch it. Post it. Pitch it. Start that project you're scared to start. You'll learn more in one messy attempt than you ever will in a thousand hours of research. Because the goal isn't to be flawless. The goal is to move, and to build momentum. The goal is to show up when it's uncomfortable, to press publish before you're 100% confident, to walk into the room even if you're not sure what to say once you get there. That's how progress works. And that's where the magic is.

. . .

If there's one thing I hope this chapter leaves you with, it's this:

You don't need to have it all figured out.
You just need to keep moving.

Perfection is a myth. It's an impossible standard that convinces you you're not ready when you are. It stops you from posting that thing, starting that business, having that conversation, or taking that risk - because you're waiting for the right timing, the right skillset, the right version of yourself. But that version? It doesn't exist. The version that gets things done is the one who starts scared and shows up anyway. I'm still learning this. Every day. I still rewrite things too many times. I still overthink my posts. I still spend hours deciding whether a font looks right or not. I still feel like I don't know what I'm doing sometimes, and then I remember, I've never known exactly what I'm doing. And that's never stopped me. I've built the things I'm most proud of in moments where I felt unqualified. Progress is messy. It looks like half-finished drafts, wobbly starts, trial and error, late-night spirals, and awkward first tries. It looks like showing up to the gym when you don't feel like it. Like recording a podcast episode for your audience of 10. Like launching a business that might flop. But every single time you choose movement over perfection, you win. Because progress stacks. It compounds. And one day, you'll look up and realise that the version of you who started, the one who didn't know what the hell they were doing, is now the one other people are learning from. So if you're stuck, if you're waiting, if you've been telling yourself "just one more tweak," let this be your nudge. You don't need to be perfect. You just need to move.

Do it before you're ready.

Say yes before you know how.

Try, fail, tweak, repeat.

This is how real growth happens. This is how you build a life that actually grows - not one that simply plateaus into mediocrity. And maybe, somewhere along the way, you'll realise that your messy, imperfect, in-progress life is actually the best thing you've ever created.

Not so quick...

If something stuck from this chapter, if a belief was challenged, or a certain thought made an impact - this is where you might want to take a second to reflect on it.

Write it down if you want to, or just sit with it for a few seconds.

Is What I Know Actually So?

Think about something you've been holding back on - the project you haven't launched, the idea you haven't shared, the message you keep rewriting.

Now, ask yourself:

Am I waiting because it's truly not ready... or because I'm afraid of someone else finding the imperfections?

Then, push even further:

If perfect was never the goal, what small, imperfect step could I take today to actually move me closer to the real goal?

LOST BUT NOT ALONE

I want to be honest with you. I'm scared to finish this book. Not because I don't believe in it. I do. With everything I have. But because it marks the end of something that's been so deeply personal, so tied to who I am and where I've been these last few years, that letting it go, releasing it into the world, feels like walking into a crowded room completely naked. And maybe that's what true purpose is - showing up anyway. Doing the thing even when you're unsure of how it will be received. Letting yourself be seen, even if you're terrified people won't get it, or worse, won't care. This book is filled with lessons I'm grateful to have learned, and a few hard truths I wish someone had told me sooner. But then again, even if someone had, maybe I needed to actually live these experiences to truly understand their value.

This book is also a mirror. I didn't write this to be a polished, perfect handbook, because that's not what life is, despite what we've been made to believe. I wrote this in real time, while I was still living it. Still figuring it out. Still working through the confusion and the pressure and the grief and the noise. So if you made it this far - thank you. Truly. It means something to me. And I hope it means something to you, too. Because if there's one thing I hope you've taken from these pages, it's this:

You're not broken.

You're not behind.

And you're not alone.

You're just human.

That's it. That's the whole thing. You are a living, breathing, feeling human who is trying their best to figure out what the hell any of this is meant to look like. And no matter how messy that looks on the outside, or how chaotic it feels on the inside, you're doing okay. Even when you feel like you're not.

. . .

I didn't write this book to give you all the answers. Quite frankly, I still don't have them. I wrote this book so I could hold up my hand and say, "Yeah, I feel it too." The same confusion. The same pressure. The same fear of being misunderstood. The same tendency to perform or pretend or overthink things that don't actually matter. The same ache for something more meaningful. The same resistance to slowing down. The same craving to feel seen.

You're not the only one.

And the truth is, most people feel the same way. They just don't say it out loud. Because we've been conned into thinking that everyone else has it all figured out. That our job is to catch up. To compare. To get it right. But that's not the point. The point is to feel it all. To let yourself be in the mess. To question things. To build something real. To love hard. To get knocked around by life and still come back to yourself at the end of it. To stay soft in a world that rewards hardness. To keep going even when it's slow or uncertain or foggy. That's what growth looks like. That's what *becoming* looks like.

. . .

You'll forget most of what you read in this book. That's just how our brain works. But if I could leave you with 5 things to remember, here they are:

1. You're allowed to feel lost.

That doesn't mean you've failed. That means you're paying attention. You're thinking for yourself. You're looking for meaning instead of just blindly following the script. That's brave.

2. You don't have to be perfect.

No one is. No one even knows what that means. Your flaws aren't bad things; they're part of what makes you human. And if you wait until you've "figured it all out" before you start living? You'll be waiting forever.

3. Stop performing.

The people in your life don't love you because you're impressive. They love you because you're *you*. They love your awkwardness, your humour, your doubts, your flaws, and they love everything else that makes you great. So please, don't hide any of it.

4. Progress is enough.

It doesn't have to be big. It doesn't have to be fast. You just have to keep moving, even if all you've got in you today is half a step. That's still something.

5. You matter.

Even when you feel invisible. Even when no one's watching. Even when your posts don't get likes, your job feels pointless, your future feels blurry, and you doubt everything. You matter. Full stop.

. . .

And one more thing: **Your story isn't over.**

No matter where you're at right now, no matter how stuck or scared or unsure you feel, you're still in it. You're still here. Still writing your next chapter, whether you can see it clearly yet or not. I hope this book gave you something to take with you as you write that next chapter. I hope it helped you feel a little less alone, a little more equipped, and a lot more okay with being human. I hope you highlighted things and dog-eared pages. Come back to it when life feels like a mess again - because it will. That's just part of the game. And I hope you remember that you don't have to do this alone. Not the growth. Not the healing. Not the figuring-it-all-out part.

This book was never meant to be the whole conversation. It was meant to be the start.

So if it helped - **pass it on to someone else.**

If it moved you - **share it.**

And if you want more - **you know where to find me.**

. . .

If I've learned anything through writing this, it's that life doesn't need to look a certain way to be meaningful. You don't need a blueprint. You just need to show up, fully, honestly, and imperfectly. That's enough. You're enough. So go. Keep building. Keep trying. Keep growing. Keep choosing your own version of this life - one messy, beautiful chapter at a time. And if no one's said it to you in a while:

I'm proud of you.

Not because you're doing everything right. But because you're still doing it, even when it's hard. That's the kind of strength the world doesn't always see. But I do. And one day, you will too...

"Maybe the journey isn't about becoming anything. Maybe it's about unbecoming everything that isn't really you, so that you can be who you were meant to be in the first place."

– Paulo Coelho

REFERENCES

Chapter 1: School Screwed You

Creativity Workshop. (n.d.). *Creative geniuses: What we can learn from a NASA creativity test.*

Eswaran, V. (2024). *From classroom to career: Building a future-ready global workforce.* World Economic Forum.

PrairieCare. (n.d.). *Perfectionism: A modern epidemic among youth.*

Chapter 2: Success Kinda Sucks

Ben-Shahar, T. (2009). *The Pursuit of Perfect: How to Stop Chasing Perfection and Start Living a Richer, Happier Life.* McGraw-Hill.

Kahneman, D., & Tversky, A. (1979). *Prospect theory: An analysis of decision under risk.* Econometrica, 47(2), 263–291.

Grandey, A. A. (2003). *When "the show must go on": Surface acting and deep acting as determinants of emotional exhaustion and peer-rated service delivery.* Academy of Management Journal, 46(1), 86–96.

Chapter 3: Whose Life Is This?

Curran, T., & Hill, A. P. (2019). *Perfectionism is increasing over time: A meta-analysis of birth cohort differences from 1989 to 2016.* Psychological Bulletin, 145(4), 410–429.

Kasser, T., & Ryan, R. M. (1996). *Further examining the American dream: Differential correlates of intrinsic and extrinsic goals.* Personality and Social Psychology Bulletin, 22(3), 280–287.

Chapter 4: Too Many Doors

Le Cunff, A.-L. (n.d.). *The affliction of abundance: FOBO or the fear of a better option.* Ness Labs.

Lally, P., van Jaarsveld, C. H. M., Potts, H. W. W., & Wardle, J. (2010). *How are habits formed: Modelling habit formation in the real world.* European Journal of Social Psychology, 40(6), 998–1009.

Chapter 5: Let It Break You

Anderson, J. (2014). *Grief is just love with nowhere to go.* [Essay widely attributed to Jamie Anderson; commonly circulated in grief literature].

Kübler-Ross, E. (1969). *On Death and Dying.* New York: Macmillan.

Kübler-Ross, E., & Kessler, D. (2005). *On Grief and Grieving: Finding the Meaning of Grief Through the Five Stages of Loss.* New York: Scribner.

Klass, D., Silverman, P. R., & Nickman, S. L. (Eds.). (1996). *Continuing Bonds: New Understandings of Grief.* Washington, DC: Taylor & Francis.

Prigerson, H. G., Horowitz, M. J., Jacobs, S. C., Parkes, C. M., Aslan, M., Goodkin, K., … Maciejewski, P. K. (2009). *Prolonged grief disorder: Psychometric validation of criteria proposed for DSM-V and ICD-11.* PLoS Medicine, 6(8), e1000121.

Shear, M. K. (2015). Complicated grief. *The New England Journal of Medicine, 372*(2), 153–160.

Chapter 6: That's Not Love

Onebright. (n.d.). *Almost 60% of men avoid sex due to performance anxiety.* Onebright.

Slotter, E. B. (2016). *Who you love changes who you are.* Psychology Today.

Chapter 7: Addicted To Likes

Social Connection Guidelines. (n.d.). *How many friends do you need?* Evidence brief. SocialConnectionGuidelines.

Chapter 8: Breaking Down Quietly

Chapman, C. (2025). *The 1% Good Club: Small Actions, Big Impact.* Wiley.

Chapter 9: No One Cares

Gilovich, T., Medvec, V. H., & Savitsky, K. (2000). The spotlight effect in social judgment: An egocentric bias in estimates of the salience of one's own actions and appearance. *Journal of Personality and Social Psychology, 78*(2), 211–222.

Mak, K. K. L., Kleitman, S., & Abbott, M. J. (2019). Impostor phenomenon measurement scales: A systematic review. *Frontiers in Psychology, 10*, 671.

Huecker, M. R., Shreffler, J., McKeny, P. T., & Davis, D. (2023). *Imposter phenomenon. In StatPearls.* StatPearls Publishing.

Chapter 10: Blow It All Up

Joo, M., & Park, S. W. (2017). *Effect of identity fusion on decision to make extreme sacrifices in romantic relationships: The moderating role of impulsiveness.* British Journal of Social Psychology, 56(4), 819–827.

Özcan, M., Çekmecelioğlu, H. G., & Konakay, G. (2025). *Reflections of self-concept clarity at work: The mediating role of psychological empowerment on the relationship between self-concept clarity and intrinsic motivation.* BMC Psychology, 13, 470.

Marshall, T. C., Bejanyan, K., & Ferenczi, N. (2013). *Attachment styles and personal growth following romantic breakups: The mediating roles of distress, rumination, and tendency to rebound.* PLOS ONE, 8(9), e75161.

Chapter 11: Perfect Is Poison

Selig, M. (2012, July 18). *The amazing power of "small wins".* *Psychology Today.*

Stockwell, B. (2025, March 14). *Breaking through perfectionism: A journey toward progress.* Psychology Today.

Enjoyed the book?

We're only just getting started...

Join the newsletter and get **Uncle Nathan's 20's Toolkit** - a free collection of templates, guides, and frameworks to help you actually find meaning in the first decade of your adult life. You'll get weekly notes on making tough life choices, enjoying your work, navigating relationships, managing your money and the occasional existential crisis survival guide.

Plus, you'll get instant access to:

- Budget template for your twenties
- Career decision-making framework
- Quarterly life review checklist
- The "Am I on track?" self-audit

Join 10,000+ readers figuring life out with us!

Scan or visit unclenathan.com/toolkit

Made in the USA
Monee, IL
08 November 2026

67384880R00090